T0113891

HIS UNIFIED WORD

A 40-Day Study Through Themes in the Old and New Testaments

LAURA WAYMACK

WestBow
PRESS®
A DIVISION OF THOMAS NELSON
& ZONDERVAN

WestBow Press books may be ordered through booksellers or by contacting:

WestBow Press
A Division of Thomas Nelson & Zondervan
1663 Liberty Drive
Bloomington, IN 47403
www.westbowpress.com
844-714-3454

All Scripture quotations are taken from The Holy Bible, New International Version®, NIV®
Copyright © 1973, 1978, 1984, 2011 by Biblica, Inc.® Used by permission. All rights reserved worldwide.

ISBN: 978-1-6642-7493-8 (sc)
ISBN: 978-1-6642-7494-5 (e)

Library of Congress Control Number: 2022914564

Print information available on the last page.

WestBow Press rev. date: 08/19/2022

CONTENTS

INTRODUCTION

On a Sunday afternoon approximately two thousand years ago, two men were traveling to a small town called Emmaus, about seven miles outside Jerusalem. Another man joined them on their journey and asked what they were discussing. They told him about the events that had recently occurred: a prophet named Jesus of Nazareth had taught among them and performed miraculous signs, but he had been arrested and executed just days earlier. That morning, the men explained, some women had found his tomb empty, but no one knew what to make of it. These two men did not realize that the stranger who walked with them was, in fact, the risen Jesus. Still unrecognized, Jesus responded, "'How foolish you are, and how slow of heart to believe all that the prophets have spoken! Did not the Christ have to suffer these things and then enter his glory?' And beginning with Moses and all the prophets, he explained to them what was said in all the scriptures concerning himself" (Luke 24:25–26). When they arrived at their destination, they suddenly recognized Jesus for who he was, and they returned to Jerusalem to tell his other followers what had happened.

This account in the final chapter of the gospel of Luke emphasizes the united story line of the entire Bible. Jesus knew that everything in the scriptures ultimately points to him. The Old Testament begins a story that culminates in the life, death, and resurrection of Jesus of Nazareth. And according to these verses in Luke, the men should have known that! So how does the Bible work? What is it about? How does it tell a story that leads to Jesus? How do passages in the Old Testament point forward to the person and work of Jesus, and how do passages in the New Testament reflect him?

Christians believe that the sovereign, all-powerful, infinite, Triune God of the universe has chosen to speak to people through the Bible. Consisting of sixty-six books in the Old Testament and New Testament, the Word of God is living and active, sharper than a two-edged sword (Hebrews 4:12). It is God breathed and useful for teaching, rebuking, correcting, and training in righteousness (2 Timothy 3:16). It is how we can know God and his plan for the world. But sometimes, the Bible can be daunting in its size and scope. Many people who desire to read the Bible struggle with knowing where to start and how it all fits together. The purpose of this forty-day overview is to provide a tool to be in God's Word consistently, reading key chapters throughout the Bible that highlight the overarching story line of creation, rebellion, redemption, and restoration. The chapters are mostly in order in the Bible, but many are skipped in between. The accompanying commentary seeks to fill in the gaps between chapters, provide connections to key themes, and offer questions for reflection and application. The teachings that go along with this study are designed to deepen our understanding of how God's Word all fits together. Ultimately, the goal of this study is for people to know God more through regular and thoughtful study of his unified Word and to see how the entire story line of the Bible leads to Jesus.

This study is designed to be done over eight weeks. Each week consists of five days of Bible study, whereby you will read the specified chapters of the Bible and the accompanying commentary. (Reading the Bible itself is the most important part; if you must skip something, skip the commentary!) You will also interact with the text in the space provided: summarizing what you have read, connecting it with bigger themes, and applying it to your own life. At the end of each week, you will also read a teaching section designed to highlight the big picture and deepen connections between passages.

Jesus explained to those two men on the road to Emmaus that all of scripture told the story of a representative who passed through death and came out the other side for the sake of a redeemed humanity. May God work richly through the depths of his Word to reveal how every part of the Bible points to Jesus, and may you know him and love him more deeply through these forty days.

READING PLAN

Day	Chapters	Overview	Day	Chapters	Overview
1	Genesis 1–2	The Creation Account	21	Luke 1–2	The Birth of Jesus
2	Genesis 3	The Beginning of Sin	22	John 1:1–18	Who Jesus Is
3	Genesis 12, 15, 17	God's Covenant with Abraham	23	Luke 4	Jesus Begins His Ministry
4	Genesis 21:1–7; 22	God's Faithfulness and Abraham's Faith	24	Matthew 5–7	The Core of Jesus's Teaching
5	Exodus 3	God Calls Moses to Deliver His People	25	John 3	God's Love for the World
		Days 1–5 Summary and Teaching			Days 21–25 Summary and Teaching
6	Exodus 11–12	The Passover and the Exodus	26	John 5, 11	Jesus's Miracles, Authority, and Power
7	Exodus 20	The Ten Commandments	27	John 15, 17	The Christian Life Defined
8	Leviticus 16	The Day of Atonement	28	Matthew 26–27	The Arrest and Crucifixion of Jesus
9	Deuteronomy 17:14–20; 18:14–22	Kings and Prophets	29	John 20	The Resurrection of Jesus
10	Joshua 1	Conquering the Promised Land	30	Luke 24	The Ascension of Jesus
		Days 6–10 Summary and Teaching			Days 26–30 Summary and Teaching
11	1 Samuel 17	David and Goliath	31	Acts 2	The Coming of the Holy Spirit
12	2 Samuel 7	God's Promises to David	32	Acts 9	The Conversion of Saul
13	1 Kings 8:1–9:9	King Solomon's Temple	33	Acts 17	Paul in Athens
14	1 Kings 18	The Prophet Elijah and the Prophets of Baal	34	Acts 26	Paul's Defense of the Christian Faith
15	2 Kings 25	The Siege of Jerusalem and the Exile of Judah	35	Romans 3	Justification by Faith Alone
		Days 11–15 Summary and Teaching			Days 31–35 Summary and Teaching

16	Psalm 89	Mourning the Fall of Jerusalem	36	Romans 7–8	Battle with Sin; Life in the Spirit
17	Daniel 3	Exiles in Babylon	37	1 Corinthians 15	The Power of the Resurrection
18	Isaiah 9:1–7 and Isaiah 53 and 61	Isaiah's Prophecy of the Coming Messiah	38	Philippians 2, Colossians 3	Christ's Example; New Self
19	Jeremiah 31	The New Covenant	39	Hebrews 8–9	Old Covenant Meets New Covenant
20	Ezra 3	Rebuilding the Temple in Jerusalem	40	Revelation 21–22	The New Heaven and Earth
		Days 15–20 Summary and Teaching			Days 36–40 Summary and Teaching

Week 1
Days 1–5

Key Themes

As you go through the five days of study and the teaching section each week, look for the introduction or development of the following themes. These themes will build throughout the Old Testament (days 1–20) and will find their fulfillment in the New Testament (days 21–40), especially in the person and work of Jesus. New themes for the week will be in **bold**.

Creation
Kingdom
Representative
Substitute
"First Gospel"
Covenant
Yahweh/Lord

1
Day

GENESIS 1–2

"In the beginning, God …" (Genesis 1:1). With these words, the unfolding story of humanity begins. In the beginning, when nothing else was there, when nothing else existed, when nothing else mattered, *God*. Later, the prophet Daniel will refer to God as "the Ancient of Days." He was there before time began, before the earth was formed, before humanity began its story. Ultimately, our story as individuals and as the human race is hemmed in behind, before, above, and below by the story of God.

"In the beginning, God created …" (Genesis 1:1). And notice *how* he created: he spoke! By the word of his mouth, light shone forth, waters separated into seas, and creatures filled the skies and land. His word brought life and emanated power.

God created something unique on each of the first three days, and then on the corresponding second three days, he filled it. Light, day, and night on day 1 were filled with sun, moon, and stars on day 4; sky on day 2 was filled with birds on day 5; seas and dry land on day 3 were filled with animals and humans on day 6. After each of these days, God declared that what he had made was *good*, and when he made man and woman in his own image, he called them *very good*. He created Adam and Eve to coreign with him over his creation and to walk closely with him. Their Edenic design included someone to love, something to do, a place to call their own, and a right and intimate relationship with their God. This was the initial design of our creation, what we were made for, what we were meant to do. These two initial chapters of Genesis set up life as it was meant to be, and the last two chapters of Revelation uniquely parallel these chapters to indicate that someday, this re-creation will be a reality and all things will be made new—again.

Notes

Read: Summarize what you read today. Write down any questions you have about the passage.

Reflect: What do you learn about God in these chapters, and/or what do you learn about people? How do these chapters contribute to the overall story line of the Bible? What key themes are introduced or developed here? (Refer to the list at the beginning of the week for help.)

Respond: What practical implications arise from God's role as Creator? How does the Word of God continue to speak light and life into your world? How do you see yourself and those around you living out—or not living out—God's Edenic design for people?

2

GENESIS 3

Today's chapter encapsulates the second part of the overarching story line of the Bible (creation, rebellion, redemption, restoration): rebellion. Adam and Eve had been designed to glorify God through enjoying a right relationship with him as their King and Creator, a right relationship with each other, and a right relationship with work and their surroundings. Tragically, in this chapter, all three of those relationships fall apart due to the conscious rebellion of Adam and Eve.

The first idea to be abandoned, thanks to the deceitful lying of the serpent, was the validity of the Word of God and the reality of judgment. In Genesis 1–2, we saw that God's word brought light and life. Here, however, we see a subtle undermining. "Did God *really* say …" (Genesis 3:1)? And we see the twisting of God's intentions. "God knows that when you eat of it your eyes will be opened, and you will be like God," says the serpent (Genesis 3:5). In other words, the serpent wants them to believe that God is withholding something good from them. He's not kind. He doesn't have their best interests at heart. Underneath the surface, God is mean and spiteful. Quite simply, he cannot be trusted.

How often do our own doubts, sins, and patterns of disbelief stem from these two fundamental errors: that God cannot be trusted and that he is not good? When we choose, like Adam and Eve did, to go our own way, we are essentially saying the same things to him. We think our plans are better than his, that his word is outdated or not to be taken seriously, and that he is not, in fact, God.

Immediately, the consequences of Adam and Eve's rebellion become evident. They feel shame at their nakedness, at the exposure of who they truly are. They cast blame and turn on each other. They try to hide from God. And then, two of the elements of God's beautiful creation, work and family, are cursed for them. Everything is marred, warped, and twisted from its original design. Relationships with God, each other, and their surroundings are no longer right. Adam and Eve are cast out of Eden, out of the good and perfect life they had been created for, due to their sin and rebellion against the God who had made them.

Yet amid this seemingly hopeless situation, a scarlet thread of possible redemption begins here and runs all the way through the rest of the biblical narrative. Tucked away in Genesis 3:15, we find what has been termed the *protoevangelion* or "first gospel." Talking to the serpent, God says, "And I will put enmity between you and the woman, and between your offspring and hers; he will crush your head, and you will strike his heel." For the rest of time, humanity would be at war with the powers of evil. The serpent, Satan, would achieve some victory against a certain person and do him some harm by "striking the heel." But this would not be the ultimate victory. There would come a day when an offspring of the woman would deal a decisive death blow to the serpent by "crushing his head." Even amid terrible rebellion and terrible consequences, God sets forth a path of hope and redemption that will one day lead straight to the cross.

Notes

Read: Summarize what you read today. Write down any questions you have about the passage.

Reflect: What do you learn about God in these chapters, and/or what do you learn about people? How do these chapters contribute to the overall story line of the Bible? What key themes are introduced or developed here? (Refer to the list at the beginning of the week for help.)

Respond: What teachings or ideas of God do you find easiest to dismiss? What aspect of the fall are you currently experiencing most tangibly? How does the "first gospel" in this chapter offer hope amid these situations?

3

Day

GENESIS 12, 15, 17

After the fall of Adam and Eve in the reading from day 2, their descendants followed in their path of rebellion. Murder entered the history of humanity when Cain killed Abel; evil rose to the point where God sent the flood, sparing only Noah and his family, and the inhabitants of the earth decided to build a tower to reach the heavens in their own ways.

Amid the chaos, God called a man named Abram (later called Abraham) to leave his home in Ur and go to a place where God would lead him. God promised that he would bless Abraham and make his descendants into a great nation, even though both he and his wife were well beyond their childbearing years. Furthermore, God said that whoever blessed them would be blessed, whoever cursed them would be cursed, and that ultimately all nations of the earth would be blessed through them. With this call began the history of the nation of Israel. Though the world was full of evil, God was setting aside a people and a nation for his own purpose. The kingdom of God would endure on earth.

Genesis 15 reflects a ritual that is strange to us but was very common in Abraham's day. Two or more parties who sought to enter some kind of covenant would "cut" the covenant, which might be similar in our time to signing a contract. The various parties involved would cut animal sacrifices in half and walk through them to indicate, essentially, "May this be done to me if this covenant is broken."

But in this passage, God put Abraham into a deep sleep and passed through the cut animals *himself* in the form of a smoking fire pot and a flaming torch. *God* was taking responsibility for his covenant with Abraham, to make his descendants as numerous as the stars in the sky and to bring him into a land to possess. *God himself* would suffer death before he allows this covenant to fail. For Abraham's part, he "believed the Lord, and he credited it to him as righteousness" (15:6).

As time went on, however, and Abraham saw no evidence of his wife, Sarah, bearing a son in her old age, he decided to take matters into his own hands and sleep with his servant, Hagar, to try to force God's promise into fulfillment in his own time and way. When God rebuked him for this, he cried out, "If only Ishmael might live under your blessing!" (17:18). Abraham wanted the blessing of God but by his own power and control. God, however, had something different in mind and promised again that the heir would come by a *spiritual promise*, not by *natural flesh*. And to reaffirm this, God instituted the practice of circumcision among the males, an outward sign of an inward covenant with and devotion to God.

From the disaster of humanity's rebellion, God would reclaim a people for himself according to a spiritual promise and would himself take the responsibility to make sure the covenant would stand. Abraham saw the first glimpses of these truths, and today we can see God's faithfulness to those promises in our own lives through the finished work of Jesus.

Notes

Read: Summarize what you read today. Write down any questions you have about the passage.

Reflect: What do you learn about God in these chapters, and/or what do you learn about people? How do these chapters contribute to the overall story line of the Bible? What key themes are introduced or developed here? (Refer to the list at the beginning of the week for help.)

Respond: What promises has God made that you either cling to or have trouble believing? How might you be trying to fulfill those promises on your own terms and in your own ways? How does this story of Abraham reflect what Jesus will later do on the cross?

4

Day

GENESIS 21:1–7; 22

Here we see the immediate fulfillment of the promise from day 3: though they are well past the age of bearing children, Abraham and Sarah have a son, Isaac. He is the first of the nation of Abraham that God promised to build. He is the indisputable evidence of the covenant, despite their continued and repeated disobedience. He is everything that Abraham and Sarah had waited for.

And then God asks Abraham to sacrifice Isaac.

Words cannot express the depths of Abraham's questions and doubt as he led his son up the mountain. "God himself will provide the lamb for the burnt offering," he reassured Isaac (22:8), but surely he wondered what God had in mind. In the New Testament, the author of Hebrews explains that "Abraham reasoned that God could raise the dead, and figuratively speaking, he did receive Isaac back from death" (11:19). But still, this was his promised heir. And after all, who would willingly sacrifice his beloved son?

Just as Abraham raised up the knife, the Lord intervened and provided a substitution in the form of a ram caught in a thicket nearby. This is one of the earliest instances of a substitutionary death—a life given in place of another life. As a result, Abraham named that place "the Lord will provide," since God had allowed something else to die in place of the original.

After all, who would willingly sacrifice his beloved son?

Notes
Read: Summarize what you read today. Write down any questions you have about the passage.

Reflect: What do you learn about God in these chapters, and/or what do you learn about people? How do these chapters contribute to the overall story line of the Bible? What key themes are introduced or developed here? (Refer to the list at the beginning of the week for help.)

Respond: How had Abraham previously experienced the faithfulness of God in his life? What sacrifice might God be calling you to make, and how does knowing his character enable you to obey? How does this story point forward to Jesus, and why does that make a difference?

5

EXODUS 3

As he promised, God chose to fulfill his promises to Abraham through the line of Isaac and Isaac's son, Jacob. Jacob (also called Israel) had twelve sons, who became the twelve tribes of Israel. One of these sons, Joseph, was sold into slavery by his jealous brothers and taken down to Egypt. In time, there was a famine in the land where his brothers were living. They had presumed him dead; however, Joseph was not only alive but was also second-in-command in Pharoah's realm. Joseph instructed his father, his brothers, and their families (seventy people in all) to come down to Egypt, and through his wise administration, he saved all their lives.

In time, these initial seventy people grew exponentially, and the land of Egypt was filled with the descendants of Abraham. A new Pharaoh arose who did not know about Joseph or his forefathers, and he enslaved the Israelites so they wouldn't become a threat to the country. Four hundred thirty years had passed since Joseph's brothers came to Egypt in search of food, and God's people groaned in anguish at their seemingly never-ending slavery.

Amid what appeared to be a hopeless situation, God called a man named Moses to rise up and lead his people out of slavery. He appeared to Moses in a burning bush and told him that he would bring the Israelites out of the land of Egypt and into the abundant and fruitful land promised to Abraham. When Moses inquired as to the name of God, he replied, "I AM WHO I AM" (v. 14)—the eternally present and faithful God who desires the full trust of his people and who always keeps his covenants. The Hebrew for this phrase provides the root of our modern term "Yahweh." God desired that this name be proclaimed from generation to generation, and when we sing of "Yahweh," we are praising his eternally immediate nature and goodness.

This God also promised Moses that he would continue to fulfill the covenant promises initially made to Abraham by bringing the people up out of slavery and out of Egypt. Although Moses was reluctant to be the one to fulfill this calling, the Lord assured him that he would accompany him with signs and wonders. In the following chapters, God will send ten plagues on Pharaoh and his people until he relents and lets God's people go. Moses will eventually lead them out of the land of slavery, give them a system by which a sinful people can dwell with a holy God, and ultimately lead them into the Promised Land.

Notes

Read: Summarize what you read today. Write down any questions you have about the passage.

Reflect: What do you learn about God in these chapters, and/or what do you learn about people? How do these chapters contribute to the overall story line of the Bible? What key themes are introduced or developed here? (Refer to the list at the beginning of the week for help.)

Respond: In what ways does the story of Moses foreshadow the story of Christ? What hopeless situation are you trusting God to bring you out of, or what has he brought you out of in the past? What are some personal implications for God's name as I AM?

Days 1–5: Summary and Teaching

These first five days of reading introduced us to the beginning of the main story line of the Bible. God created all things and called humans to be in perfect relationship with him, ruling and reigning together with him over his good creation. But instead, Adam and Eve chose to rebel against God's rule, and they tried to create a world where they alone could define good and evil. Their relationships with God, each other, and the world around them were permanently twisted. As a result of their sin, they could no longer be in the presence of God, so they were banished from the Garden of Eden. But in God's gracious plan, this wasn't the end of the story. He offered seeds of hope even amid judgment, and he began to work anew through the patriarch Abraham and his family. He chose them in order to accomplish his redemptive purposes in the world, but this section ends with the nation of Israel enslaved to an oppressive foreign power. In this section, I will offer a few more thoughts on each passage from this week, and I will explore connections between the passages and some overall themes and ideas that we can trace as the story line of the Bible begins to unfold.

We begin with Genesis 1–2, the first chapters in the Bible and the setup to the entire story, and it is here that we see God for the first time. Consider the *purpose* of these chapters. They are primarily *theology*, intended to give the nation of Israel a glimpse into the God who had redeemed them out of Egypt. The original audience had just been liberated from a pantheon of powerless gods in Egypt and now stood at Mount Sinai, awaiting explanations on what just happened and instructions on what happens next. The ancient nations of Egypt and Babylon all had their own accounts of creation, and they would usually include multiple gods fighting against one another or against elements of darkness or chaos. In the end, the winner would barely emerge victorious and therefore hold a tentative reign over the world. But this account told of *one* God—unheard of in the ancient Near East—and his mighty acts of creation, from nothing, with no struggle. He simply spoke, and it happened. And everything that he created was *good*.

These chapters can teach us a great deal about the nature of God, his purposes for creation, and his plan for the world. God comes first, and he is separate from the created order; he makes everything, but he himself is unmade. This rejects atheism, pantheism, materialism, and the foundations of many other worldviews. Additionally, God speaks. He is not an impotent, silent being; he is fundamentally a communicator. Ultimately he will be revealed in his Word (see John 1:1–18). And God created, introducing the idea of accountability. If he made the world and everything in it, then the world and everything in it owes him their allegiance and will answer to him. Finally, God made humanity in the image of God, the *Imago Dei*, and both the man and the woman reflect him and reign over creation with him. Humanity was given stewardship over creation. God freely shared the privilege of ruling and reigning alongside him.

These initial chapters of the Bible are so much more than a simple origin story of a local deity. They set up the person and character of God and establish what his kingdom was initially supposed to be like. They set the stage for everything else that happens in the biblical story. Time and again, stories and themes will echo the garden, a place where heaven and earth were truly united, with Adam and Eve as priests—mediators between God and creation—and corulers with God himself. The name Eden means "delight," and it was here that God delighted in the goodness of his world and humanity delighted in the goodness of their God.

All of this, however, would soon come undone. In just the third chapter of the Bible, the fall of humankind wreaked havoc on the whole of creation. And this was not a passive fall; rather, this was a willful rebellion, a revolution against the Creator God. This seven-times-declared-good creation was now marred by broken relationships between individuals and between people and God. The fall ushered in shame and doubt, blame and pride, and ultimately physical and spiritual death. None of these were what God intended. None of these were "natural" parts of creation and existence. None of these were meant to be. We can only truly understand the gravity of sin by understanding its solution: the death of the Son of God. And we must see the significance of this passage for the rest of the biblical canon. We cannot agree on the gospel if we cannot agree on what it seeks to solve.

The deceitful repulsiveness that characterized the first temptation began with a question about what God *really* said or *really* meant. It introduced just the right amount of possibility and skepticism, and it smuggled in the assumption that God's Word is subject to our judgment. Eve responded somewhat wisely at first but included exaggerations of her own; already she was buying into the idea that God is the cosmic party pooper, and this led to unbelief and distrust. Then in the serpent's response, the first doctrine to be denied was the doctrine of judgment. The climax of the passage is a lie big enough to mess up existence, where God becomes an enemy and a rival. Satan encouraged the woman to "take and eat." And as biblical scholar Derek Kidner has said, "So simple an act; so hard its undoing. God will taste poverty and death before 'take and eat' become verbs of salvation."[1] In this act, Adam and Eve chose to define good and evil for themselves instead of allowing their good God to set forth the parameters of his own creation, and the results were disastrous.

The initial consequences that erupted from the first temptation and sin included the expulsion of Adam and Eve from the garden. In this, we see the tragic truth that humanity could no longer dwell in the place of God because of sin. Yes, God provided a covering for their nakedness and shame, but that covering was necessary for the first time. Both God's wrath and God's grace are revealed simultaneously; let us not abandon one. But here too, in this chapter of brokenness, is one

---

[1] Derek Kidner, *Genesis: An Introduction and Commentary* (Chicago: InterVarsity Press, 2008), 73.

tiny thread of hope: the protoevangelion, or "first gospel" of Genesis 3:15, which sets the stage for Jesus's triumph over all death and evil forever.

In his excellent book *Far as the Curse is Found*, theologian Michael D. Williams uses an analogy of an acorn and an oak, emphasizing both what *currently is* and what this idea will *grow to become* throughout the rest of the biblical story.[2] The acorn is the *current reality* of the text, what the original audience would have known. So here in Genesis 3, God is declaring war on the serpent, on the one who brought rebellion and darkness into the world. The battle will employ an offspring of the woman. This offspring shall receive a wound ("you will strike his heel"), but the snake will receive a fatal blow ("he will crush your head"). But the oak is the *ultimate reality* of the text, what we can see today through the history of scripture. The idea of an offspring, or "seed," will continue with the promises to Abraham, and in the New Testament, Paul will explicitly connect this Seed to Christ (see Galatians 3:16). This idea of the acorn and the oak is crucial to seeing how God has told one unified story in his Word and designed everything to ultimately point to Jesus.

The genealogies that follow in the next chapters of Genesis lead us next to one particular seed of the woman: Abraham. This Abraham was chosen by God to begin the nation of Israel, and it is with Abraham that we see the beginnings of the language of covenant. (In the ancient Near East, a covenant signified a specific relationship between individuals, nations, or entities.) In this covenant, God makes several extraordinary promises to Abraham, including a seed or offspring—a continuation of the idea just seen in Genesis 3:15. This seed would be protected by God himself, would become a new nation (eventually Israel), and would occupy the land of Canaan. This land was not chosen simply as fertile farmland, as isolation, or for protection; rather, it was an intentional choice as a doorway to the world. God's promises to Abraham were not only for his family and for his eventual nation but for the entire world, since in the original covenant promise, Israel was blessed *in order to* be a blessing to the nations around them. Speaking more broadly, we can say that this covenant involved God's people, in God's place, under God's rule, living for God's purpose. This had been the original intent of Eden as well, and throughout the Bible, we can see how all of the story seeks to establish this ultimate perfection.

In Genesis 15 and 17, despite all odds, God reaffirms his covenant with Abraham multiple times, even in the face of impossibility. Seed? Abraham was almost one hundred years old, and his wife was barren. Blessing? These people seem more like a curse as Abraham keeps lying about his wife and bringing curses on other nations. Land? Abraham was a seminomadic wanderer all of his life, as were the next several generations. The covenant seemed like a disaster from the beginning. But in Genesis 15, *God himself* was the one who walked through as the covenant was cut. God alone is responsible for keeping his promises. And he will see it done.

And so, in Genesis 21—when Abraham was one hundred years old—he and Sarah had a son, Isaac. God had finally proved faithful! But then, in Genesis 22, God asks Abraham to sacrifice his

---

2 Michael D. Williams, *Far as the Curse Is Found: The Covenant Story of Redemption* (Phillipsburg: P&R Press, 2015).

son. This must have been unbearably heartbreaking and confusing for Abraham, for not only was Isaac a long-awaited and beloved son, but he was also the promised heir—from the mouth of God himself! Would Abraham be willing to sacrifice what God himself had promised? For Abraham, this was his ultimate test of faith and the climax of the story of his life. Until this moment, God had made promises again and again, and Abraham had taken matters into his own hands again and again. God told him to stay in Canaan; he went to Egypt and deceived the rulers by calling his wife his sister, almost bringing disaster upon them all. God told him to wait for an heir through Sarah; he sexually abused his maidservant Hagar to produce a son he later rejected. So now, at the end of his life, what would he do? Back in Genesis 15:6, it says, "Abraham believed God, and it was credited to him as righteousness." Would he continue to believe God now, in the face of an unimaginable request? Would he continue to look to God and believe that he would fulfill his promise even if Isaac was killed? Could the covenant still be fulfilled?

Abraham trusted God and did what he asked, though he doubtless had no true idea what was happening or why. But at the last moment, God provided a ram—an essential *substitute*—that ultimately points forward to Christ. Perhaps we wonder what kind of God would ask someone to sacrifice his only son, especially when in other parts of the Old Testament this kind of child sacrifice to pagan gods was expressly and thoroughly forbidden. Without knowing all of the answers, we know that this was the very God who was willing to sacrifice his. And later, we see that Abraham is honored for believing amid impossible circumstances and against all odds (Hebrews 11:1, 8–12, 17–19).

Before we leave this first great patriarch behind, consider the acorn and the oak in the covenant from the story of Abraham. The acorn, or what the biblical authors would have seen and understood, showed God's faithfulness over the next several generations. Abraham and Sarah miraculously had a son, Isaac, who miraculously had two sons, Jacob and Esau. Then Jacob miraculously had twelve sons, who became the twelve tribes of the nation of Israel. The Promised Land would come in about five hundred years when Israel took possession of the Promised Land of Canaan in the book of Joshua. And they certainly had the blessing of God. God would protect Israel through slavery, famines, droughts, and exile, never leaving them or forsaking them. The initial promises of a great nation, a great name, and a great blessing were already coming true.

But none of this permanently fulfilled the promise of God's people in God's land under God's rule. The Old Testament is filled with stories of the nation of Israel repeatedly turning their backs on God. The covenant should have been shattered. But instead, we see God himself fulfilling the covenant just as he promised. The oak tree that we can now see had its beginnings in the acorn of the Abrahamic covenant, but it went so much further. In Matthew 1 and Luke 1, the "seed" of Abraham is traced through generations all the way to Jesus Christ himself. *Jesus* was the ultimate blessing to all of the world. He brought about the advent of the *true* "Promised Land," where God brings us out of our slavery to sin and into a land ruled by God himself, a place of rest and joy through no merit of our own. In Exodus 19:6, Israel would be described as "a kingdom of priests and a holy nation." In the New Testament, we, the church, are also described as "a chosen people, a royal priesthood, a holy nation, a people belonging to God, that [we] may declare the praises of him who called [us] out of darkness into his wonderful light" (1 Peter 2:9). And through all of this, these promises are based on *God's* faithfulness, not ours. He has walked through. Indeed, he *was* "cut in two" yet remained faithful to his promises.

God remained faithful through the generations of Abraham, Isaac, and Jacob. When Jacob's son Joseph was sold into slavery in Egypt by his jealous brothers, he ended up saving his family and his nation, and at the end of the book of Genesis, about seventy Israelites moved down to Egypt. Not long afterward, a new pharaoh felt threatened by the rapidly growing nation of Israel and enslaved them for four hundred years. Were the promises forgotten? Had God abandoned his people? When all hope seemed lost, God called Moses to lead his people out of slavery and into the Promised Land.

When God called Moses in Exodus 3, he first responded with skepticism and essentially asked, "Who am I, that I should do this, and who are you, that we should believe that this will happen?" God's response in Exodus 3:14–15 is utterly outstanding. "I AM WHO I AM. This is what you are to say to the Israelites: 'I AM has sent me to you.' God also said to Moses, 'Say to the Israelites, "The LORD, the God of your fathers—the God of Abraham, the God of Isaac, and the God of Jacob—has sent me to you." This is my name forever, the name by which I am to be remembered from generation to generation.'" Not only is this God linking himself to the promises of the patriarchs that we just looked at, but he is also providing an identity for himself.

The Hebrew for "I AM" comes down to four letters: YHWH, or our word *Yahweh*. Whenever we see the "LORD" in small capital letters in the Bible, it indicates that this is the word used, and it is a version of the verb "to be." It means I AM. It means HE IS. It means that the present tense is always true of God. Early in Genesis, a more general term for God is used: Elohim. But as soon as Genesis 2, Yahweh is used alone or with Elohim, as translated "the LORD God." Yahweh is the personal and covenant name of God, emphasizing his role as Israel's redeemer and covenant Lord. Both names are used thousands of times in the OT, and often together, leaving no doubt as to the God to whom the author refers: Israel's God, the "LORD." So it is *this* God, the covenant God, the one who goes back generations, who promises to be with Moses as he goes to confront Pharaoh. In fact, in Exodus 3:12 when God tells Moses, "I will be with you" before Moses asks his name, the "I will be" there is the *same* word as the "I AM" in verse 14.

Abraham's situation was unique in that he was called by this God into a strange land and a new faith out of nothing. Everyone since him, however, including Moses here, has the promises of God to look back on. Very intentionally, YAHWEH is the covenant name for God. *I am the one who keeps promises. I am the one who has done, and am doing, exactly what I said that I would.* While the statement is an amazing expression of *presence*, it is also more than that. It is one of *action*. Much like in the creation story, this God is set apart especially from other gods. God wanted Israel to not only hear his words but to see his actions and therefore trust him as the true YAHWEH Elohim. He does not offer empty promises; he has tied himself eternally to his covenant and reveals his true nature through what he does and how he acts on behalf of his people. This covenant Lord will continue to reveal himself throughout the rest of the narrative of the Old Testament.

This week, we have seen God create the earth out of nothing and declare it good. We have seen his kingdom established on earth with Adam and Eve as his representatives on earth. But they failed, leading to a broken world and a fallen human race. We saw God's righteous judgment alongside his unmerited grace as we looked at the first hint of the gospel in Genesis 3:15. Later, God sovereignly chose Abraham and promised to make him into a great nation in order to be a blessing to the rest of the world. God would uphold this covenant against all odds, in the seemingly impossible circumstances. He would be faithful to Abraham, Isaac, and Jacob, though they themselves would not see the final results of those covenant promises. And finally, he would declare to Moses that as Israel's covenant God, he would bring his people out of slavery and into the Promised Land. In these stories, we see both the acorn and the oak of how God is working in the patriarchs as well as how he is starting threads that will carry to the cross and beyond.

Next week, we will see God's pattern of redemption in the Exodus and the Passover. We will see his system of laws, priests, sacrifices, and kings designed to allow a sinful people to dwell in the presence of a holy God. Most of all, we will see a God who, despite the failings and faithlessness of his people, always keeps his promises and maintains his faithfulness to his covenant from generation to generation.

Days 6–10

Key Themes: As you go through the five days of study and the teaching section each week, look for the introduction or development of the following themes. These themes will build throughout the Old Testament (days 1–20) and will find their fulfillment in the New Testament (days 21–40), especially in the person and work of Jesus. New themes for the week will be in **bold**.

Creation	**Redemption**
Kingdom	**Passover Lamb**
Representative	**Holiness (law)**
Substitute	**Priest**
"First Gospel"	**Sacrifice**
Covenant	**King**
Yahweh/Lord	**Prophet**

6
Day

EXODUS 11–12

The last plague is alarmingly severe and incredibly significant. God sends a destroying angel to kill the firstborn son of every household. Not only would this be an unspeakable personal loss for each household, but this would also effectively decimate the nation of Egypt, as dreams and inheritances were bound up with the firstborn. How can we begin to reconcile this tragic scenario with what we know of a loving, just, and merciful God?

Three points may help us to wrap our minds around this situation. First, Moses, the one who is speaking to Pharaoh on behalf of God at this point, is alive only because of his mother's willingness to break the law: Pharaoh's law that *every baby boy* born to the Israelites had to be thrown into the Nile River and killed (Exodus 1:22). Second, this is not the first plague or the initial way that God revealed himself to the Egyptians. This is the *tenth* clear and incontrovertible demonstration of power by an almighty God over the national gods of Egypt. Each time, the individual plague was intended to cause Pharaoh's heart to be softened and let God's people go out of slavery, but each time, Pharaoh refused. Third, the covenant relationship between Yahweh and Israel is often portrayed as a father-son relationship. Yahweh had seen his beloved son enslaved by a cruel and oppressive nation for over four hundred years, and he was going to rescue him. As the Lord instructed Moses to say to Pharaoh, "This is what the Lord says: Israel is my firstborn son, and I told you, 'Let my son go, so he may worship me.' But you refused to let him go; so I will kill your firstborn son" (Exodus 4:22–23). As in the flood, and as we will see later with the exile and ultimately the crucifixion of Jesus on our behalf, a righteous and just God brings rightful judgment upon rebellion and sin.

In his mercy, God made a provision for Israel and allowed one life to substitute for another. The only way the Israelites could be spared was to spread the blood of a lamb on their doorpost. The blood of this lamb would allow the destroying angel to pass over that household, since a sacrifice had been made on their behalf. The Israelites were to prepare a specific meal laden with significance, including "bitter herbs" to remind them of the bitterness of slavery and "bread made without yeast" to allow them to leave in haste (v. 8). This meal was so significant that immediately God decreed that this day would be commemorated every year as a lasting ordinance and reminder of what God had done. And that very night, after 430 years in slavery, God used Moses as his mediator and spokesperson to lead his people out of slavery.

This event of the Exodus and the Passover became a critical staple of memory and faith in the lives of the Israelites. Historical books, prophets, and psalms all refer back to this event regularly as a reminder of what God had done. As the crucifixion and resurrection of Christ are the focal point of salvation history for New Testament believers, the Exodus and Passover were the focal point of salvation history for Old Testament believers. Ultimately, Jesus himself would become our Passover Lamb, allowing another's life to be substituted in place of our own (1 Corinthians 5:7). And it would again be through the blood of a Lamb without defect: the firstborn son of God.

Notes

Read: Summarize what you read today. Write down any questions you have about the passage.

Reflect: What do you learn about God in these chapters, and/or what do you learn about people? How do these chapters contribute to the overall story line of the Bible? What key themes are introduced or developed here? (Refer to the list at the beginning of the week for help.)

Respond: How would you explain the tenth plague to someone uncomfortable with the idea of God killing the Egyptian firstborns? What elements of the Exodus and the Passover are reflected in the lives of believers today? How is Christ our Passover Lamb?

7

Day

EXODUS 20

Today's reading brings us to the Ten Commandments. These straightforward, seemingly simple rules have formed the basis of moral codes for countless societies, both pagan and religious. But before we gloss over today's reading, let us consider the context and its implications.

Some pretty amazing things had happened in the lives of the Israelites. God used Moses to speak powerfully to Pharaoh for the release of his people. When Pharaoh refused, God sent ten plagues on Egypt in order that his people might be freed (Exodus 7–11). The Passover feast was established, showing that the blood of a lamb would save the people (Exodus 12), and the Israelites left Egypt with Pharaoh's permission. But then, Pharaoh changed his mind and pursued the Israelites to the Red Sea, where God miraculously parted the waters and destroyed the oncoming enemy army. After praising the Lord and rejoicing in his great wonders for them, Moses and the Israelites came to Mount Sinai, where Moses received the Ten Commandments here in Exodus 20.

The second verse of this chapter sets up the rest of it in its rightful place. "I am the Lord your God, who brought you out the land of Egypt, out of the house of slavery." God has just performed a great series of miracles in order to bring his people out of bondage. He rescued them, he redeemed them, and he called them into a community that would follow him. These commandments are to govern the way that this community lives.

Note that God did not set up these commandments so that the people could earn his favor and therefore be rescued or somehow reach God. No, the people already *had* God's favor, he had *already* rescued them—through no merit of their own—and now they were to live accordingly. Moreover, these commands were for the good of the Israelites, and subsequently for us. Imagine a society that completely operated according to these standards. That was the goal for God's people as he set up the structure of what his kingdom's life would look like.

But these Ten Commandments reveal something uncomfortable amid this. No matter how "good" of a person we are or strive to be or how obedient we are to a loving God, we have all broken something in these commandments. On the average day, we can't even make it past the first one, which says, "You shall have no other gods before me" (v. 3). How many things and people do we place in front of God? The Ten Commandments were set forth as a covenant between God and his people, as instructions for how to act as a redeemed people. And the reality is we have all broken that covenant. These external rules and regulations show us the way to live, but we can't do it on our own. We need an internal change in order to fulfill these commandments and to love God the way we so desire to. We need to be fixed at a level so deep that we can't even reach it.

But God knows that. And once again, he takes it upon himself to fulfill *our* part of the covenant. (Look back to day 3 for yet another time he did this.) In Ezekiel 36:26–27, God promises, "And I will give you a new heart, and a new spirit I will put within you. And I will remove the heart of stone from your flesh and give you a heart of flesh. And I will put my Spirit within you, and cause you to walk in my statutes and be careful to obey my rules."

The Ten Commandments are *good*. And they are a response to what God has already done. But even then, when we cannot follow them completely, we have a Savior who transforms our hearts and lives, giving us the power to walk in his ways, to serve him, to know him, and to love him.

Notes

Read: Summarize what you read today. Write down any questions you have about the passage.

Reflect: What do you learn about God in these chapters, and/or what do you learn about people? How do these chapters contribute to the overall story line of the Bible? What key themes are introduced or developed here? (Refer to the list at the beginning of the week for help.)

Respond: How does the order of God's redemptive events in Exodus change our relation to his commandments and laws? How does the story of the exodus and of Moses's role as mediator mirror that of Jesus? How are our lives being transformed, or not transformed, in obedience to the laws of God?

8
Day

LEVITICUS 16

From the beginning, God had desired a personal relationship with Israel, and he had made gracious covenants with Abraham and Moses in order to allow this to happen. But the Ten Commandments cast a spotlight on the inability of the people to keep his statutes. Even as Moses was receiving the law of the Lord from God himself, the people were turning their jewelry into a golden calf to worship! The perfect holiness of God was simply incompatible with the utter sinfulness of his people.

In order to maintain both his own holiness and the relationship with his people, God established the system of laws, priests, and sacrifices that are found throughout the book of Leviticus. To the people of Israel, this was a gracious manual of regulations enabling a holy King to set up his throne among a sinful people. It gave parameters and guidelines for how to practically live a life that was set apart for God, as he had called them to be. Throughout the book, spiritual holiness is symbolized by physical perfection in the priests, the people, and the animals used for sacrifice—all of which points forward to the perfect sacrifice of the spotless Lamb of God.

The priests, in particular Aaron (Moses's brother) and his sons, were charged with the sacred duty of mediating between the people and God. Everything from their garments to their sacrifices was explicitly outlined so that they could serve God well. A few chapters before today's readings, two of Aaron's sons had tried to make sacrifices and enter the presence of God in their own way, contrary to the commands of God, and they were immediately killed (Exodus 10:1–3). The presence of God Almighty was not to be taken lightly or presumed upon in *any way*, by *anyone*.

The Day of Atonement, described in great detail in Leviticus 16, specified the correct way to enter the presence of God in the sacred place within the tabernacle known as the Most Holy Place or the Holy of Holies. This inner room was to be entered only once a year, and the guidelines laid out here were to be followed to the letter. The high priest (and *only* the high priest) could enter only after purifying himself and making sacrifices for his own sins. He then offered the sacrifice of a goat on behalf of the sins of the people and released another symbolic goat into the wilderness to carry the sins far away from the people. He then had to purify himself again before rejoining the people. Chapter 17 goes on to explain why blood was so important. "For the life of a creature is in the blood, and I have given it to you to make atonement for yourselves on the altar; it is the blood that makes atonement for one's life" (v. 11). This Day of Atonement was the most significant ritual for dealing with the sins of both the priest and the people in the presence of a holy God.

If these ordinances and prescriptions seem overwhelming, consider the role of Christ. He was both perfect sacrifice and perfect priest. He did not enter the presence of God "by means of the blood of goats and calves; but he entered the Most Holy Place once for all by his own blood, having obtained eternal redemption" (Hebrews 9:12). Consider how great the sacrifice of Jesus, if by one act he fulfilled and replaced an entire system of priests and laws. And consider how in *both* instances the desire of God was to—amazingly—dwell with his people by any means necessary.

Notes
Read: Summarize what you read today. Write down any questions you have about the passage.

Reflect: What do you learn about God in these chapters, and/or what do you learn about people? How do these chapters contribute to the overall story line of the Bible? What key themes are introduced or developed here? (Refer to the list at the beginning of the week for help.)

Respond: How are the detailed specifics of these chapters in Leviticus an act of mercy? What makes the Day of Atonement different from any other day? Why is it so significant in the lives of the people of Israel? How does Jesus exemplify both perfect priest and perfect sacrifice?

9
Day

DEUTERONOMY 17:14–20; 18:14–22

After Moses led the people of Israel out of slavery in Egypt in the Exodus, they came to the brink of the Promised Land of Canaan that God had spoken of to Abraham so long ago (see day 3). But because of sinful unbelief, doubt, and fear, the people refused to go into the land (see Numbers 13–14). They rebelled against Moses and threatened to stone him, and they rebelled against God and complained that they wished they were back in Egypt. The Lord, understandably frustrated, said to Moses, "How long will these people treat me with contempt? How long will they refuse to believe in me, in spite of all the miraculous signs I have performed among them?" (Numbers 14:11). As a consequence of their rebellion, the people were sent away to wander in the wilderness for forty years. A new generation would be the one to inherit the Promised Land.

Here in our chapters in Deuteronomy, those forty years of wandering are almost finished. Moses is repeating the law to the people before they enter Canaan, reminding them of the God who brought them out of slavery and into his glorious presence. He also offers up a few new specifics for their life under God's rule in God's land. The reading for today establishes guidelines for two new future offices: the office of king and the office of prophet.

Even as Moses gives instructions about the king, he notes that the people will initially want a king to be like all of the other nations (17:14). Nevertheless, a few indicators will be necessary. He must be "the king the Lord your God chooses" and one "from among your own brothers," not a foreigner (v. 15). He must not acquire great wealth for himself, take many wives, or return to Egypt for additional assets. Above all, he must write a copy of the entire law for himself and "read it all the days of his life so that he may learn to revere the Lord his God" (v. 19). Likewise, the prophet needs to be one from among the people as well. The Lord explains, "I will put my words in his mouth, and he will tell them everything I command him" (18:18).

Both offices of king and prophet were intended to mediate between God and the people in specific ways. They needed to be leaders among the people, pointing them continually back to their covenant Lord. As the people enter the land of Canaan and move into the time period of the judges, kings, and prophets, keep these offices in mind. Some people will fill them wholeheartedly, some will try but fall short, and some will openly abandon the requirements of office. Soon, the need will become evident for a true King and a true Prophet, one who will perfectly exemplify what it means to lead the people and follow God, speaking and ruling on his behalf for the good of the nation.

Notes
Read: Summarize what you read today. Write down any questions you have about the passage.

Reflect: What do you learn about God in these chapters, and/or what do you learn about people? How do these chapters contribute to the overall story line of the Bible? What key themes are introduced or developed here? (Refer to the list at the beginning of the week for help.)

Respond: Why do you think the Israelites rebelled against God just before entering the Promised Land, despite everything they had seen and experienced? In what ways do you tend to do the same thing? How might the offices of king and prophet be significant in the biblical story line?

10

JOSHUA 1

Generations before Moses, God had promised Abraham that he and his descendants would live in the Promised Land. He renewed that promise to Isaac, Jacob, and Moses. When Moses led the people out of Egypt, they were on their way to inhabit that land. However, due to the people's sin and rebellion, God declared that the generation that had come out of slavery in Egypt would not see that good land. Instead, they wandered in the desert for forty years. God took care of them in miraculous ways during this time, such as feeding them with manna from heaven and guiding them by his presence in the tabernacle. But Moses and the generation of Israelites who followed him would die before entering the land that God had promised to their forefathers.

When Moses died, a new leader arose in Israel: Moses's former aide, Joshua. He would be the one to lead God's people across the Jordan River and into the land God had designated for them. Here in the first chapter of Joshua, we see God's encouragement and challenge to Joshua and then Joshua's subsequent encouragement and challenge to the people. The land God had promised was occupied by other tribes who did not worship the one true God. Their lifestyles and cultures were marked by sexual sin, child sacrifice, and idol worship. Joshua and the army of Israelites would have to drive out these various peoples in a series of battles that probably seemed terrifying to the people. A few tribes of Israel—the Reubenites, the Gadites, and the half-tribe of Manasseh—would eventually occupy land outside the boundaries that God had set for the Promised Land, but they too were to go in with their brothers until they found rest in the land.

There, on the banks of the Jordan River as they prepare to cross and fight for God's kingdom, God tells Joshua to live by his laws and to be strong and courageous. "Do not let this Book of the Law depart from your mouth; meditate on it day and night, so that you may be careful to do everything written in it. Then you will be prosperous and successful. Have I not commanded you? Be strong and courageous. Do not be terrified; do not be discouraged, for the Lord your God will be with you wherever you go" (vv. 8–9). God's Word and laws were to guide them, and his presence would strengthen them as they entered this new and unfamiliar territory.

The remainder of the book of Joshua details how God led the people of Israel to occupy this land. The evil in the land was driven out, and the good rule of God led the people to their promised rest. However, the next book of the Bible, Judges, shows us how temporary this rest was, because the people were still full of sin and rebellion. One greater than Joshua was needed. And when Jesus—whose name is the Greek form of the name Joshua, meaning "the Lord saves"—came, he completed what the first Joshua had started. Jesus, like Joshua, came up out of Egypt (see Matthew 2:13–23) and fulfilled the purpose that God had called him to. And Jesus, like Joshua, overcame the powers of evil and brought God's people into rest. But unlike Joshua, Jesus doesn't bring his followers to a physical and temporary place of peace but to one of eternal and permanent rest (see Hebrews 4:1–13).

Notes

Read: Summarize what you read today. Write down any questions you have about the passage.

Reflect: What do you learn about God in these chapters, and/or what do you learn about people? How do these chapters contribute to the overall story line of the Bible? What key themes are introduced or developed here? (Refer to the list at the beginning of the week for help.)

Respond: How can God's Word and God's presence guide you as you enter new and unfamiliar territory in your life? What evil is God calling you to fight against and drive out in your own life or in the world? In what ways does this part of the Old Testament narrative foreshadow what is yet to come in the person and work of Jesus?

Days 6–10: Summary and Teaching

Last week, we looked at the good creation of God, including man and woman, and their subsequent rebellion. We saw how God immediately set in place a path for hope through the offspring of that woman. We saw God's righteous judgment and his hatred of anything that separates his creation from him, and we saw how he worked in and through the patriarchs Abraham, Isaac, and Jacob to begin to enact his covenant promises. Finally, we read about the nation of Israel in slavery in Egypt and how Yahweh, Israel's covenant God, called Moses to lead his people up out of Egypt.

This week then, the story continued. Moses instructed the Israelites to observe the first Passover meal and then led them out of Egypt in Exodus 11–12. He then gave the law of God to the people in Exodus 20. Several elements of the case law soon followed: the sacrificial system and Day of Atonement in Leviticus 16–17 and instructions about kings and prophets in Deuteronomy 17–18. Finally, we saw God's promise to Abraham fulfilled in Joshua 1 as the Israelites took possession of the Promised Land. As we dive into these passages, let's remember the order in which they occur and the ways that Yahweh continues to keep his covenant promises to Israel for the sake of the world.

After the covenant Lord had instructed Moses to lead his people out of Egypt, there came the challenge of getting Pharaoh to agree to the plan of letting his free labor force go without a second thought. When Pharaoh refused, God used Moses to bring ten plagues on Egypt. The plagues on Egypt deliberately put Yahweh in a ring against the gods of Egypt. The sacred Nile River was turned to blood; the goddess Heqet, represented by a frog, was mocked by an infestation of frogs; Isis and Seth, agricultural gods, were overwhelmed by hail and bad crops; and even Ra himself was thwarted when darkness covered the land.

After Pharaoh's continued refusal despite devastation to his land, crops, and reputation, the Lord announced the tenth and last plague that would now devastate his nation and his family. The firstborn of every family would die. Not only would this loss be felt personally, but the nation as a whole would be severely crippled as dreams, inheritances, and plans for the future were often wrapped up with the firstborn. Back in Exodus 4:22–23, before any of the other plagues had begun, God had told Moses that this was his endgame. "Then say to Pharaoh, 'This is what the Lord says: Israel is *my* firstborn son, and I told you, "Let my son go, so he may worship me." But you refused to let him go; so I will kill *your* firstborn son'" (emphasis mine). There was a special significance for the firstborn since the nation of Israel was to God like a firstborn son.

However, amid this act of righteous judgment, God again made a provision. A lamb without defect could be sacrificed instead, and when the people put the blood of the lamb on their doorframes, the angel of the Lord would "pass over" that house and the firstborn would be spared. This event was so significant that it was to be repeated year after year in remembrance of this miraculous event. Then, just as God had promised, Moses led the people up out of Egypt in the event that would come to be known as the Exodus.

It is nearly impossible to overstate the significance of the Exodus throughout the rest of the Bible. Every subsequent event in the Old Testament looks back to the Exodus, and it is the one event that is assumed by every writer. Psalmists, prophets, and chroniclers look back to this event as the central act of redemption, and it is listed as the most spectacular example of God's redemption before the cross (see Judges 19:30; Hosea 13:4; Jeremiah 7:25, 23:7–8). The nation of Israel even dated itself from this point (1 Kings 6:1). This was Yahweh, the covenant God, acting not on the merit of his people but on the unconditional and unearned promises to Abraham, Isaac, Jacob, and Moses. This was an incredibly visual and practical display of God's power and his sovereignty even over the most powerful nations. And it unequivocally called out a people for himself, a nation that would be his people in the world: the people of Israel.

Last week we discussed how many passages of the Old Testament can be read at two levels. One is the level that would have been known and experienced by the original audience, or the analogy of the acorn. Their experience would be rich but more limited than ours is today. It is important for us to see the acorn to put ourselves in their shoes. However, living on this side of the resurrection with the added benefit of the rest of scriptures, we can also see the oak, or the ultimate reality to which these things point.

What the people now knew—the acorn—was that their lives had been spared because another had been sacrificed. They also knew that somehow, the blood of the animal was enough for God to accept. They also knew that they had been redeemed and impossibly brought out from deepest slavery and bondage. This set a pattern that the New Testament would pick up on immediately, that Jesus would speak of directly, and that we as the church would come to remember and celebrate on a weekly basis.

Before he even began his ministry, John the Baptist called out Jesus as "the lamb of God, who takes away the sin of the world" (John 1:29). Peter says that we are redeemed "by the precious blood of Christ, a lamb without blemish or defect" (1 Peter 1:19). Paul explains to the church at Corinth that "Christ, our Passover lamb, has been sacrificed" (1 Corinthians 5:7). Jesus and his disciples were eating the Passover meal on the night he was betrayed, and the bread and the cup that became our weekly communion would forever be linked to the blood of the lamb on that Passover night.

Furthermore, this account of redemption from bondage leading to sanctification in covenant and the establishment of God's kingdom—all through the ministry of a chosen mediator—directly parallels the gospel message. Theologian Graeme Goldsworthy explains it this way:

Possession of the Promised Land and the freedom to be the people of God is not a matter of simply walking over the border into the kingdom of God, and much less is it something we are born into. The Israelites, even as the chosen people, are by nature aliens and strangers to God's kingdom because they are Adam's children outside of Eden. God chose to reveal his redemptive purposes in the context of Israel's history. Thus the captivity in Egypt and the exodus demonstrate the captivity of the human race to the powers of evil, and the necessary powerful work of God himself to rescue people from that awful slavery. When God the warrior fights for his people against the enemy, victory is certain.[3]

For generations, millennia after the Exodus, the people of Israel and the people of God would continue to celebrate this truth.

After bringing the people out of Egypt, God declared that Israel was to be a "kingdom of priests and holy nation" (Exodus 19:6). Priests were those designated to mediate between God and men. "Holy" indicated separate from but not *separated* from. The world and the other nations needed to be able to see Yahweh in their midst. So in order to do this, God continued to follow the covenant formula. He even used the language and setup of a common historical covenant introduced by the Hittites, called a suzerain-vassal treaty, in order for the people to better understand their relationship. As seen in Exodus 20:1, it is important to note that the relationship always came *before* the stipulations. The law wasn't given *in order to form* a relationship but because a relationship *already existed*.

This is worth restating, because we so often get it wrong. The Exodus, the redemption, the relationship, came *before* the law. The law was never intended as an alternative way to God; rather, the law presupposed the historical action of God, and the law guides and nourishes our covenant relationship with God. Deuteronomy 10:12–19 is worth quoting at length here, because it reminds us of the true purpose of the law.

> And now, Israel, what does the Lord your God ask of you but to fear the Lord your God, to walk in obedience to him, to love him, to serve the Lord your God with all your heart and with all your soul, and to observe the Lord's commands and decrees that I am giving you today for your own good? To the Lord your God belong the heavens, even the highest heavens, the earth and everything in it. Yet the Lord set his affection on your ancestors and loved them, and he chose you, their descendants, above all the nations—as it is today. Circumcise your hearts, therefore, and do not be stiff-necked any longer. For the Lord your God is God of gods and Lord of

---

[3] Graeme Goldsworthy, *According to Plan: The Unfolding Revelation of God in the Bible* (Downers Grove: InterVarsity Press, 1991), 136.

lords, the great God, mighty and awesome, who shows no partiality and accepts no bribes. He defends the cause of the fatherless and the widow, and loves the foreigner residing among you, giving them food and clothing. And you are to love those who are foreigners, for you yourselves were foreigners in Egypt. Fear the Lord your God and serve him. Hold fast to him and take your oaths in his name. He is the one you praise; he is your God, who performed for you those great and awesome wonders you saw with your own eyes. Your ancestors who went down into Egypt were seventy in all, and now the Lord your God has made you as numerous as the stars in the sky.

Given all that the sovereign Lord had done for the nation of Israel—from creation until the Exodus—and how much he loved them, obedience to the law was a way that they could love him in return and experience the good that he desired for them.

We might tend to see laws or rules as restrictive, unnecessarily prohibitive, or legalistic. But scripture itself has a different view. Again and again, the psalms praise the law of God as good, life-giving, and supremely valuable (see especially Psalm 19 and Psalm 119). These Ten Commandments, and the specific case laws that followed, allowed a redeemed people to walk in fellowship with God. The Ten Commandments also match up to the "law in our hearts" (our consciences) as well as laws and rules from other cultures. There is a reason for this. Again and again, the purpose of the law is stated so that we can love God and "that it may go well with you" (Deuteronomy 6:18, 4:40, 5:33, 6:24, 12:28, 30:15–20). There is no area—public life, private life, family, business, sex, politics, or religious activity—to which God's rule does not extend. Psalm 119:32 sums it up nicely. "I run in the path of your commands, for you have set my heart free."

Many aspects of the subsequent law code were specific to the theocratic nation-state of Israel, including the priests and kings that we will see in the next passages, and the significance of the law to our lives today can be confusing. Reformer John Calvin summed up three purposes of the law as relevant to the Christian: the law as a mirror to show our sinfulness in light of God's holiness, the law as a restraint of evil in a fallen world, and the law as a revelation of what is pleasing to God. The law could not change hearts or save people, but in general, a redeemed people will live a transformed life, and these laws, beginning in Exodus 20, indicated what that transformed life would look like for the nation of Israel. In the law, we can also see grace as a holy God commits himself to a sinful people and teaches them how such a relationship can even be possible.

Under the Mosaic law, priest and sacrifice went hand in hand, as seen in Leviticus 16. Aaron, as the leader and forefather of the priests, was responsible for making the sacrifices appropriate for the situation. The Bible, and the book of Leviticus in particular, discusses several different types of offerings and sacrifices to be made for various occasions, such as worship or the need for ceremonial cleanliness. This part of the law—which we no longer observe today, thanks to the ultimate sacrifice of Christ (as we will see later in the book of Hebrews)—explains how Israel is to be God's holy people and how they are to worship him in a right and holy manner. Spiritual holiness is symbolized by physical perfection in both people and animals. Here too we find the key idea of a substitution, or a life for a life.

The Bible first introduced the idea of a sacrifice—something given in place of another—when God made coverings for Adam and Eve way back in Genesis 3. Noah, Abraham, Isaac, and Jacob all made sacrifices to God before the Mosaic law was put in place. Passover, including the key idea of substitutionary atonement, had already been explained and was set in place as a yearly reminder of what God had done for them. Here, in the Day of Atonement, we see the idea of a substitution twice—first, in that an animal was sacrificed for the sins of the people, and second, that one of the animals was set free to carry that sin away. Before the priest could do this, however, he had to make a special sacrifice for himself so that he could be pure to serve the role of making the people pure.

The analogy of the acorn and the oak can be used again in understanding the sacrificial system. In the acorn, we see that sin is present and must be dealt with, since we have a holy God. In order to deal with this sin, death is required (sin is *that* serious). But a system is set in place so that one life can be offered in place of another life. This system is broken and imperfect and requires daily or yearly repetition, but by God's mercy, it made the people outwardly clean.

In the oak then, we also see that sin is present and must be dealt with, since we have a holy God. In order to deal with this sin, death is required (sin is *that* serious). But a system is set in place so that one life can be offered in place of another life. For us, ultimately, this is Jesus. But there is a key difference. "Unlike the other high priests, he does not need to offer sacrifices day after day, first for his own sins and then for the sins of the people. He sacrificed for their sins once for all when he offered himself" (Hebrews 7:27). On the second-to-last day of this study, we will look at Hebrews 7–9, which will fully unpack this oak and explain how Jesus is both the ultimate high priest *and* the ultimate sacrifice, cleansing us not just on the outside but from the inside out. This is how great Jesus is. By one act, he fulfilled for all time what others had to practice day after day, year after year, for centuries. If this chapter felt overwhelming or confusing to you, allow that to point you to the greatness of the sacrifice of Jesus!

Two other themes are set up in Deuteronomy that are worth looking at briefly: kings and prophets. Kings are a provision in the law several hundred years before Israel actually becomes a kingdom in the earthly sense of the word—with a human king. This king would need to fear the Lord and lead his people well by being one of them, by not amassing great wealth for himself, and by reading his own copy of the law of the Lord all the days of his life. It is worth noting that the king could not also be a priest under the Mosaic law. Next week, we will see how the first kings, Saul, David, and Solomon, compared to these instructions.

Prophets are another provision in the law that allows someone to come into the midst of the people with a special word from God. This person would speak to God on behalf of the people and to the people on behalf of God—somewhat like a priest but from more of a teaching perspective than a sacrificial perspective. The test of prophets given here is in the fulfillment of their words. If they speak in the name of the Lord and what they say doesn't happen, they are false prophets and are later strongly condemned by God. This sets the stage for prophets to follow Moses, such as Elijah, Isaiah, and Jeremiah.

These offices are set in place for the good of the people, to help them know the Lord and live in peace and holiness before him. Many people will fill these roles throughout the Old Testament. Some filled them well and pointed the people back to God; others filled them poorly and led the people astray. If we are still looking from the acorn to the oak here, we may start to see just how many roles Jesus ultimately fulfilled, including ultimate king and ultimate prophet.

Finally, we return to the story of Israel. Due to the continual sin of the people and leaders of Israel, including Moses, God did not lead them immediately into the Promised Land of Canaan. These people had seen the ten plagues, the Exodus, and the parting of the Red Sea with their own eyes, yet they did not believe. God decreed that this particular generation would not enter the Promised Land; rather, it would be their children who entered after forty years of wandering in the desert.

When Moses died, God called his second-in-command, a man named Joshua, to be the one to actually lead the people into the land promised to Abraham so many centuries earlier. God urged courage and promised success *if* (and already this is a big *if*) Israel obeyed the laws of God that had been given to them. As it stood, pagan nations and people groups who practiced child sacrifice and who generally hated God's laws occupied the land, so the people of Israel were called to take possession of it. Over the book of Joshua, these nations would become symbolic of the powers of evil and darkness that the kingdom of God would drive out.

Three major things occur in this chapter: God calls and addresses Joshua; Joshua, as the new leader, addresses Israel; and Israel responds in kind. But in this, we see something bigger, a high point in the history of Egypt and the culmination of nearly everything since Eden. God called his people, redeemed them out of slavery, gave them new laws to live by, and brought them into the Promised Land. Put another way, he made Abraham a great nation, he blessed them, and he called them into their land—exactly what he had said centuries earlier in Genesis 12. This land was not paradise, but it would be a taste of God's rule over God's people in God's land. God had been faithful to Israel. The question that we are left with after this week is this: would Israel remain faithful to him?

Between last week and this week, we have seen God at work from creation until the brink of Canaan. He created everything and called it good, and his kingdom was in place. But humankind rebelled against him. From that point, God enacted a plan. He promised to destroy the powers of evil through an offspring of the woman. He called Abraham to begin his people based on no merit of his own. He continued working in the lives of Isaac, Jacob, Joseph, and the people in Egypt. The nation went from one man to seventy and then hundreds of thousands in just a few hundred years.

God then powerfully and graciously redeemed them out of slavery in Egypt, gave them the law to indicate how a sinful people could dwell with a holy God, and instituted systems of sacrifices, priests, kings, and prophets for their good. Finally, he led the people into the Promised Land of Canaan under the leadership of Joshua. In all of these parts, we see elements of later truths: Jesus as the true priest, the true sacrifice, the true king, and the true prophet. We see hints of the gospel in the idea of redemption from slavery and a call to live a holy life. And we see how God is continuing to enact his plan through human history.

Next week, we will see how God uses King David and the temple to further his kingdom on earth, but we will also see how Israel rebels against their covenant Lord again and again. Amid their sin, God will preserve a remnant, for he will continue to be faithful to his promises.

Days 11–15

Key Themes: As you go through the five days of study and the teaching section each week, look for the introduction or development of the following themes. These themes will build throughout the Old Testament (days 1–20) and will find their fulfillment in the New Testament (days 21–40), especially in the person and work of Jesus. New themes for the week will be in **bold**.

Creation	Redemption	**David/Son of David**
Kingdom	Passover Lamb	**Jerusalem**
Representative	Holiness (law)	**Tabernacle/temple**
Substitute	Priest	
"First Gospel"	Sacrifice	
Covenant	King	
Yahweh/Lord	Prophet	

11
Day

1 SAMUEL 17

After the previous reading in Joshua 1, God led the people of Israel in battle against all the evil nations residing in the Promised Land, and the people experienced a temporary rest. Soon, however, they entered a downward spiral through a cycle of rebellion. The people would turn away from God, and he would bring punishment on them through oppression by other nations. Then the people would cry out to God, and he would bring a deliverer through an appointed judge. Finally, the people would turn back to God for a short time before rebelling again—and so goes the book of Judges. Everyone did what was right in his own eyes, and the book ends on a bleakly horrific note that shows just how far the people had fallen from the good rule and design of God.

In time, the people decided that the judges weren't working for them anymore, and they decided to ask their leaders for a king—as Moses had told them they would back in Deuteronomy 17 (day 9)—so that they could be like the other nations around them. The prophet Samuel warned against this, explaining that a king would use and abuse the people and their resources, but Israel insisted. God tells Samuel, "They have rejected me [God] as their king" (1 Samuel 8:7), so he instructs Samuel to anoint a man named Saul.

Saul was everything a king should have been for Israel: physically imposing, socially impressive, and from the right tribe and the right family. He led the people in battles against their enemies and pretended to follow God's commands. His heart, however, was not right with God, and his continual disobedience and rebellion led God to reject him as king over Israel.

In his place, God anointed a young man named David, who would become the archetypal king of Israel and serve as a foreshadow of King Jesus. In contrast to Saul, David did not appear very kingly, but God reassured Samuel, "The Lord does not look at the things man looks at. Man looks at the outward appearance, but the Lord looks at the heart" (16:7). In chapter 17, we see David bravely fight against Goliath because he knew that the battle belonged to the Lord. And so began the good reign of King David.

David's reign was far from perfect. His lack of discipline and control over his household led to strife and rebellion throughout the kingdom. He had to continually be on the run from King Saul's murderous schemes against him. His affair with Bathsheba defined him as a lying, adulterous, hypocritical murderer. Yet in spite of this, David would later be known as a man after God's own heart. Many of the psalms were written by David, so we see a glimpse into his true desire to follow after the Lord and his commands. David's psalms and songs take us throughout the entire range of human emotion and experience, and in it all, we see the echoes of the young man who stood up, against all odds, to fight the terrifying powers of evil in the world in the power of God alone—and won.

Notes
Read: Summarize what you read today. Write down any questions you have about the passage.

Reflect: What do you learn about God in these chapters, and/or what do you learn about people? How do these chapters contribute to the overall story line of the Bible? What key themes are introduced or developed here? (Refer to the list at the beginning of the week for help.)

Respond: What does it look like in our world today when people do what is right in their own eyes? What is the difference between how people judge others and how God judges others? What can the story of David reveal to us about how God works in and through the lives of sinful people?

12

2 SAMUEL 7

Part of King David's fully devoted heart for the Lord shows up in this chapter. After achieving victory over his enemies on all sides, David realized that he was living in comfort, while the God of Israel was still housed in a temporary tabernacle. So he decided to begin plans for a permanent temple, a house for the Lord. The prophet Nathan seemed to think it was a good idea, so he gave his blessing.

Before the plans could begin, however, God came to Nathan in a dream and instructed him to tell David the complete opposite. God said that he had never dwelt in a temple before and that David would not be the one to build it now. Rather than *David* building a house for *God*, *God* declared that he was going to build a house for *David*. What God meant by this wordplay was that he was going to build a household, or dynasty, for David. He stated clearly, "The Lord declares to you that the Lord himself will establish a house for you: When your days are over and you rest with your fathers, I will raise up your offspring to succeed you, who will come from your own body, and I will establish his kingdom. He is the one who will build a house for my Name, and I will establish the throne of his kingdom forever. I will be his father, and he will be my son" (vv. 11–14). David rejoiced in this promise and worshiped God in a beautiful prayer throughout the rest of 2 Samuel 7.

As we look forward in the story line of the Bible, we see that the *immediate* fulfillment of this promise is in Solomon, David's biological son who succeeded him on the throne and built the temple (see day 13). But the language here reaches even further. The line will continue unbroken and David's dynasty will continue *forever*. How can this be?

This is one of many places in the Old Testament where the current, historical situation has both *immediate* and *ultimate* fulfillment, like we saw with Abraham, Moses, and Joshua. Solomon would carry on the line of David and build the temple in the next generation. But several hundred years later, another descendant of David would come: Jesus, the one with a throne that will continue *forever*.

Within the next several generations, the nation of Israel would break apart into the kingdoms of Israel and Judah. Both would see a revolving door of kings, many of whom were incredibly evil and led the people astray through the worship of idols. Family after family after family took over the kingdom of Israel, lasting only a king or two before God deposed them from the throne. But the kingdom of Judah saw David's line unbroken until the exile. Despite sinful ways and evil kings, "for the sake of his servant David, the Lord was not willing to destroy Judah. He had promised to maintain a lamp for David and his descendants forever" (2 Kings 8:19). And then, with the coming of Jesus, David's line remains unbroken *forever*, and he will build the *true* house of God.

Notes
Read: Summarize what you read today. Write down any questions you have about the passage.

Reflect: What do you learn about God in these chapters, and/or what do you learn about people? How do these chapters contribute to the overall story line of the Bible? What key themes are introduced or developed here? (Refer to the list at the beginning of the week for help.)

Respond: What characteristics of God are shown through his covenant with David? In what ways is this covenant ultimately fulfilled in Jesus? When has God done something in your life that caused you to respond, like David, in absolute awe and thankfulness?

13

1 KINGS 8:1–9:9

As King David grew old and neared his death, his son Solomon took over the throne. He was probably only about twenty years old and was doubtless overwhelmed at the prospect of leading an entire kingdom. So when God graciously offered to give him anything he desired, he didn't ask for wealth or power; he asked for wisdom. God was pleased with this request and gave him wisdom, and he also gave him what he had not asked for in riches, power, and wealth.

Then, several years into King Solomon's reign, he fulfilled his father David's initial plan and built a temple for God, a permanent dwelling where his presence could reside. Solomon's prayer of dedication is worth savoring. In front of the whole kingdom, Solomon declared, "O Lord, God of Israel, there is no God like you in heaven above or on earth below—you who keep your covenant of love with your servants who continue wholeheartedly in your way. You have kept your promise to your servant David my father" (8:23–24). Once again, God's faithfulness in keeping his promises is on full display.

Solomon continued. "But will God really dwell on earth? The heavens, even the highest heavens, cannot contain you. How much less this temple I have built!" (8:27). Solomon was under no false pretenses that this elaborate building of wood and gold, built by man, could actually contain the full glory of the God of the universe. Rather, this temple would be the focal point of worship for the God of Israel—an earthly palace for a heavenly king. His presence was manifest there in the Ark of the Covenant and in the Most Holy Place, but he certainly wasn't confined by walls or buildings. Solomon was amazed that God would even dwell among his people at all!

The rest of his prayer acknowledged that the people would sin and that there would be trouble and hurt and pain throughout the kingdom. But when these things happened, Solomon prayed that God would hear the cry of his people and turn and forgive them. Solomon also prayed that no matter what, God's name would be made great among the nations and that the people of Israel would commit their hearts to the Lord. God responded by reaffirming his promise to David's son, just as he had done generations earlier to Abraham's son.

But the temple does not last forever. The people do not remain committed to God. His name is not revered among Israel and among the nations as it should be. Many years down the road, the symbolic presence of God will even depart from this temple, indicating that God is temporarily leaving his covenant people to their own sinful ways (Ezekiel 10). Yet God's promise to David and to Solomon remains.

In the New Testament, the bodies of Christians are called the "temple of the Holy Spirit" (see 1 Corinthians 3:16–17; 6:19–20). Just as the eternal and uncontainable God condescended to have his presence reside with Israel in the temple built by Solomon, so we too have the presence of God residing with us. May we never take this lightly!

Notes

Read: Summarize what you read today. Write down any questions you have about the passage.

Reflect: What do you learn about God in these chapters, and/or what do you learn about people? How do these chapters contribute to the overall story line of the Bible? What key themes are introduced or developed here? (Refer to the list at the beginning of the week for help.)

Respond: If you were in Solomon's position, do you think you would have asked for wisdom? What elements of wisdom and justice can you see in these chapters of Solomon's reign? How are Solomon's temple and our own bodies related, and how might this affect our lives?

14
Day

1 KINGS 18

In yesterday's reading, King Solomon began his reign in wisdom and justice. However, whereas his father, David, had had a whole heart for God, Solomon had more like half of a heart for God. The other half was reserved for his wives and their gods—seven hundred wives and three hundred concubines, to be precise, each with her own religion and customs that led him away from the one true God. As a result, when Solomon's son Rehoboam ascended to the throne, another leader, Jeroboam, also arose, and the nation was divided into two distinct kingdoms: the southern kingdom of Judah (led by descendants of David and comprised of the tribes of Judah and Benjamin) and the northern kingdom of Israel (led by various family lines and comprised of the other ten tribes). Many of these leaders of both the northern and southern kingdoms led the people into idolatry and progressively worse sin over the years, and the books of 1 and 2 Kings and 1 and 2 Chronicles narrate the decline of the nation of Israel until, finally, God exiled them.

Occasionally though, God raised up a prophet or king to call his people back to him. One such prophet was Elijah, who served during the reign of one of Israel's most abhorrent kings, Ahab. Because Elijah spoke the truth of God's Word and denounced evil King Ahab's sinful ways, Ahab and his wife, Jezebel, hated him and sought to kill him on multiple occasions. So when he challenged Ahab to a public confrontation, the stage was set for a dramatic showdown.

Elijah called for the prophets of Baal, a popular pagan god, to go up against the one true God. Because Baal was thought to be an incredibly powerful deity in control of elements, such as rain and fire, Elijah told them to set up a sacrifice and call on Baal to light it with fire from heaven. He taunted and teased them as the sacrifice remained unlit throughout hours of empty ritualistic frenzy. Elijah then repeated the situation for himself and his God, except that he had the sacrifice doused with water to make it even more impossible. But when he called on the name of the God of Abraham, Isaac, and Jacob, the fire came down and consumed the sacrifice, the wood, the stones and soil, and the water around the altar! Verse 39 has the people proclaiming in awe, "The Lord—he is God! The Lord—he is God!"

This powerful, vindictive, and dramatic display of God's power is inspiring, encouraging, and fist-pumpingly awesome. But it can also cause us to wonder why God doesn't do this more often. He is God! Why doesn't he prove it? Why doesn't he rain fire down and perform miracles and prove beyond the shadow of any doubt that he is the true ruler of the universe?

But in the words of theologian D. A. Carson, "The most shocking thing about this confrontation is that it was needed. These are the covenant people of God."[4] Ultimately, even this dramatically victorious showdown between God and the false prophets did not permanently turn back the hearts of the people to their true and rightful King. The Lord is God, but as 1 Kings 19 shows us, sometimes we see him best not in earthquakes or powerful winds but in whispers. And our hearts must be willing to see him for the King he is.

---

[4] D.A. Carson, *For the Love of God: A Daily Companion for Discovering the Riches of God's Word* (Wheaton: Crossway Books, 1998), 315.

Notes

Read: Summarize what you read today. Write down any questions you have about the passage.

Reflect: What do you learn about God in these chapters, and/or what do you learn about people? How do these chapters contribute to the overall story line of the Bible? What key themes are introduced or developed here? (Refer to the list at the beginning of the week for help.)

Respond: How have you seen God act powerfully in your life or in the lives of those you know? Why do you think that God doesn't often act this dramatically today? Why were the people of Israel ultimately not loyal to this God, despite his clear displays of power and might?

15
· Day ·

2 KINGS 25

After Elijah's demonstration of God's power in yesterday's reading, the kings of both Israel and Judah continued to lead their people astray. They worshiped idols, sinned against the Lord, and broke his covenant again and again. Finally, in approximately 740 BC, the northern kingdom of Israel was taken into captivity by the Assyrians (see 2 Kings 17), the result of the implementation of the covenant curse given to Moses way back in Deuteronomy 28 and 32. The southern kingdom of Judah lasted a few more generations because of some godly kings, but ultimately they too were taken into captivity by the Babylonians in approximately 586 BC.

When the kingdom of Babylon, led by King Nebuchadnezzar, finally overtook Jerusalem, it was a devastating scene. Homes were burned, the temple was ransacked, and the people were carried away from their Promised Land. All of this happened because of the sin of the people of the nation of Israel. For generations, God had given chance after chance after chance, but to no avail. They had broken the covenant with their God again and again and again, so God remained faithful to that same covenant and exiled them from the land.

Yet here in a bleak ending to the books of the Kings, due to the direct result of the people's sin, we find an unexpected bit of hope. Normally when a nation was overtaken by another, the king was the first to be killed. This was often done in a ceremonial or symbolic way that was further humiliating to the nation that had been captured. The lack of a leader demonstrated once and for all that the nation as they knew it was done. But here, Jehoiachin, the last king of Judah, is not killed. Rather, he is treated with kindness and even eats at the king's table with an allowance as long as he lived.

Admittedly, this is an odd bit of hope and a strange ending to the historical book. But first, 1 and 2 Kings was most likely written by one of these Judahite exiles, explaining to the people their history and how they got to where they are now. To those readers, this would have left it open-ended. Perhaps not *all* hope was lost, as it most certainly seemed. And in consideration of the overall story line of the Bible (creation, rebellion, redemption, and restoration), most of these books clearly highlight the "rebellion" aspect. Yet these last verses offer a glimpse into redemption. Even amid untold sin and direct covenant breaking, God had a remnant in mind: a group of people who would one day return to the Promised Land. Although the human side of it was beyond repair, God wasn't done with these people yet.

Notes

Read: Summarize what you read today. Write down any questions you have about the passage.

Reflect: What do you learn about God in these chapters, and/or what do you learn about people? How do these chapters contribute to the overall story line of the Bible? What key themes are introduced or developed here? (Refer to the list at the beginning of the week for help.)

Respond: When in your life have you felt overwhelmed by your own failings and sin, perhaps finding yourself in a place beyond hope because of what you had done? How does this chapter offer a glimpse of the hope of the gospel that is our solution today?

Days 11–15: Summary and Teaching

Last week, we saw that all of the initial promises of God to the patriarchs were fulfilled. God had promised Abraham that he would have countless descendants, a nation, a covenant God, and a land to call his own. Finally, after decades of impossibilities, centuries of slavery, and generations of wanderers, the nation of Israel was redeemed from Egypt and brought into the Promised Land of Canaan under the leadership of Joshua. Just before he died, Joshua reminded the leaders of the people, "You know with all of your heart and soul that not one of all the good promises the Lord your God gave you has failed. Every promise has been fulfilled; not one has failed" (Joshua 23:14). The same Yahweh who made the initial promises carried them through to fulfillment.

Just before they entered the Promised Land, Moses gave these final instructions to the people, in what we know today as the Shema, meaning "Hear" or "Listen carefully and obey," and what Jesus later quotes as the greatest commandment:

> Hear, O Israel: The Lord our God, the Lord is one. Love the Lord your God with all your heart and with all your soul and with all your strength. These commandments that I give you today are to be upon your hearts. Impress them on your children. Talk about them when you sit at home and when you walk along the road, when you lie down and when you get up. Tie them as symbols on your hands and bind them on your foreheads. Write them on the door frames of your houses and on your gates. When the Lord your God brings you into the land he swore to your forefathers, to Abraham, Isaac, and Jacob, to give you—a land with large, flourishing cities you did not build, houses filled with all kind of good things you did not provide, wells you did not dig, and vineyards and olive groves you did not plant—then when you eat and are satisfied, be careful that you *do not forget the Lord,* who brought you out of Egypt, out of the land of slavery. (Deuteronomy 6:4–12, emphasis mine)

God knew their tendency, which is often the same as ours: to forget. And unfortunately, this week we look at a time period that can be summed up by Israel saying, in effect, "We forgot."

This week, we looked at the period of the kings. We saw Israel's new kingship in action when David fought Goliath in 1 Samuel 16–17. We saw God's renewed covenant to the house of David in 2 Samuel 7. And we saw David's son, Solomon, build a permanent temple for the Lord in

Jerusalem in 1 Kings 8–9. Then we looked at one example of how the prophet Elijah stood up to unfaithfulness and reminded the people who the true God is in 1 Kings 18. Finally, we watched as the sinfulness and idolatry of the kingdom of Judah came to such a head that God used foreign nations to send them into exile in 2 Kings 25. As we dig deeper into some of the key themes from these chapters, let's remember that the unfaithfulness to the covenant was always on the part of the people and *never* on the part of God. The one who made the promises—and upon whom the covenant rests—is *always* faithful.

The Israelites took full possession of the land of Canaan throughout the book of Joshua, bringing the kingdom of God into an alien and rebellious world. This was designed to be God's rule in God's land. The relationship with the covenant Lord was fully established. The Lord is perfect, and the law is perfect. But unfortunately, things did not go according to plan, and what was lacking was the people's response.

After the death of Joshua, the nation entered the period of the judges. As a scattered people group in a new land, they were susceptible to invading nations around them in terms of both military and religion. The agrarian gods of the people of Canaan were collectively called Baals. The people of Israel continued to worship Yahweh as their god of history, but they had had no experience with him as a god of creation or a god of crops. All around them, they saw nations performing fertility rites and having sex with temple prostitutes to honor and glorify their Baals, and their crops were succeeding. So they started to combine the two. They never fully rejected their covenant God. Instead, they just went back and forth between gods as the need arose. When celebrating the Passover, they turned to Yahweh, but when celebrating harvest, they turned to the Baals.

This created a downward cycle of sin, servitude, supplication, and salvation. Israel would turn to other gods, and in fulfillment of the more negative side of the covenant promises, God would give Israel over to foreign powers. After a time of oppression, the people would cry out to God, and Yahweh would raise up a judge to save Israel. This spiral continued through many generations and led Israel into a significant downfall as a nation. Finally, when the Philistines invaded—a more powerful army than the new nation had yet seen—and stole the Ark of the Covenant, the people demanded a monarchy to have a more unified nation and to be like all the other nations. Their initial demands for a king were inherently misguided; they were flat out rejecting God's rule as king. But God redeemed the demands and set up a structure that would one day lead to the *ultimate* king.

The first king who was anointed was a man named Saul. He was everything a king should be, by frail human standards: tall, handsome, and a military leader. He was *not*, however, intended to be the sole covenant mediator or representative. He was under the law of God, and the priests and the prophets performed their unique and separate functions alongside the king as a balanced system to keep the wayward nation under the law of God. Soon, however, in the face of military defeats, Saul became everything that a king shouldn't be. Last week we discussed the necessary characteristics of a king in Deuteronomy 17, which were set in place well before the kingship was established. The ideal king was supposed to follow God, to lead the people well, to avoid amassing wealth for himself, and to honor the roles of priest and prophet. In the span of a couple of chapters of 1 Samuel, Saul did the opposite of all of these things. And because he rejected the Word of God, God rejected him as king, and in his place, God raised up a man named David, which brings us to our familiar passage of David facing Goliath.

If Saul was what a king "should" be in the eyes of the people but not in the eyes of God, David was exactly the opposite. He was not what a king should be in the eyes of the people, but he certainly fit the bill in the eyes of God. In a bit of an awkward moment, David was anointed as the true king while Saul still reigned; the passage even goes so far as to say that the "spirit of the Lord came upon David" and "departed from Saul" (1 Samuel 16:13–14). When David volunteered to fight Goliath in 1 Samuel 17, we see that David was what a king was truly meant to be. In verse 47 of the familiar account, David said to the Philistine giant, "All those gathered here will know that it is not by sword or spear that the Lord saves; for the battle is the Lord's, and he will give all of you into our hands." The ironic thing here is that the people knew no such thing at this point. For weeks they had been terrified of this Philistine champion and refused to do anything about it out of fear. They assumed that sword and spear would, in fact, save them, so when they proved insufficient, they had nowhere else to turn. David, however, showed true kingship. As one man, he represented the nation, and he pointed them back to the true victor, the Lord, and this begins a pattern of the reign of God represented on earth by the reign of David and his family.

Once David's kingship was fully established, he established Jerusalem as the capital of the nation and brought the Ark of the Covenant to rest there. Back in the book of Exodus, just after Moses gave the people the Ten Commandments, God had instructed that a tabernacle be built. This was the gracious means by which the mediators, or priests, could access God. No detail of its design or construction was left to the imagination, because they needed God to tell them exactly what their relationship with him would look like. There were three great truths inherent in the construction of the tabernacle. God wills to dwell with his people, sin separates a holy God from those people, and God himself provides the means of reconciliation.

The tabernacle was a temporary dwelling place for God. The wandering Israelites would carry it with them, and they would set it up at the center of their camp when they settled somewhere. But wherever it went, it was the tangible presence of God with them, especially represented in the Ark of the Covenant. So when David moved the ark permanently to Jerusalem, he desired a permanent dwelling rather than a tent. And this is where we pick up in 2 Samuel 7, one of the greatest covenant chapters of the Bible.

David realized that after years of military successes, he was now established in a safe, permanent home, and he told the prophet Nathan that he wanted to build a house for God. Instead of the tent flaps of the tabernacle, he wanted to build a home for God and for his Ark of the Covenant in a more elaborate and permanent temple. The prophet initially agreed to this request, seeing nothing wrong with it whatsoever. But that night, God responded to the request in a completely new way. David wanted to build a house (or a temple) for *God;* God said no thanks and responded by promising that *he* would build a house (or a dynasty) for *David*. He promised to establish his lineage, his throne, and his kingdom *forever*.

This language is so startling that David responds in utter amazement, "Who am I, O Sovereign Lord, and what is my family, that you have brought me this far? And as if this were not enough in your sight, O Sovereign Lord, you have also spoken about the future of the house of your servant. Is this your usual way of dealing with man, O Sovereign Lord?" (2 Samuel 7:18–19). God has just promised that his—*David's*—throne would endure *forever*. God did not need David to build him a house. What could he offer God that he did not already own?

When we look at the language of vv. 12–16, it immediately invites a reading of the acorn and the oak. This is also a prime example of why so many Old Testament passages that *point* to Jesus are not immediately *about* Jesus. In other words, the acorn matters. Verse 14 says that the son of David will also be a son of God. While it may be easy to see Jesus in this passage, this idea of sonship was much more about the identity of the person and who they were identified with. He also says that "when he does wrong, [God] will punish him with the rod of men," but that his "love will never be taken away from him." In the immediate context, this is of course *not* talking about Jesus, since we know that Jesus never sinned. Rather, he is promising a dynasty that, even when there is wickedness, will not be utterly destroyed. It will be punished, but it will not be annihilated or removed from the throne. The promises will stand.

But even in this acorn, the language is too far-reaching to simply be about an earthly succession of kings. God says that "your house and your kingdom will endure forever before me; your throne will be established forever" (v. 16). Later, the psalms will pick up on this theme as clearly Messianic. Another king will come, from the line of David, who will restore the kingdom of God. "Son of David" becomes a term used to describe not only earthly kings from that line but also of the coming Messiah, the coming Anointed One who would be the ultimate hope of the people.

David, and subsequent earthly sons of David, will continue to represent God's rule on earth through their kingship, for better or for worse. In our last chapter for this week, we see that the earthly line of David will indeed be punished, but it will not ultimately be destroyed. The prophets, particularly Jeremiah and Ezekiel, will speak of a new David ruling in a new Jerusalem (both of which are serving as types or models). So when Jesus—a direct descendant of David—is born in the city of David, or Bethlehem, this Davidic covenant is in view (Luke 2:4). When sick people cried out for Jesus's miraculous healing by addressing him as "Jesus, Son of David," this Davidic covenant is in view (Luke 18:38). And when they hang the sign on the cross that Jesus was "the King of the Jews," even in mockery, this Davidic covenant is in view (Luke 23:38). Jesus, great David's greater Son, will reign forever, and *his* kingdom will have no end. Once again, in the covenant to David, we see that God was immediately at work in the life of one family for the sake of the nation, but that its *ultimate* fulfillment would be found in the *ultimate* king, who remains so forever because of his death and resurrection, indicating the power of an indestructible life.

Meanwhile, David's initial idea was picked up by his son, Solomon. Using his unprecedented wisdom, Solomon built an intricate and ornate temple to be the central focus of religious and spiritual activity in Jerusalem. This was also a unique and powerful symbol of God's presence with his people. After Solomon's dedication prayer, the Lord reaffirmed his covenant to the son of David, promising to establish his throne and his lineage forever.

The Lord also reaffirmed another part of the covenant that had been true from the beginning as well: the conditional aspect. Redemption had never been about simply escaping from bondage. There had always been the component of a new life in a new land with a new king. Israel was saved by free grace and unconditional election, and God would remain faithful to his promises. However, accompanying the covenant were always choices: the way of life or the way of death, the way of covenant blessings or the way of covenant curses. The Old Testament speaks often of this reality that blessings and responsibility go hand in hand under the covenant (e.g., Deuteronomy 28–30). Yahweh, Israel's covenant God from the beginning, is the one true God, and he—rightfully!—will not share his glory with another, particularly with idols. After Solomon, the prophets will speak again and again of both the Lord's faithfulness and the dangers of unbelief. The covenant is sure, but the blessings are not.

And sure enough, after Solomon, the kings began to turn away from God. In the generation after Solomon, the kingdom actually divided into two: the northern kingdom of Israel and the southern kingdom of Judah. The kingdom of Israel saw kings from various families and lineages, and it quickly spiraled down into idolatry and sin. Throughout this time, prophets spoke to the nation and to the kings about returning to the Lord their God. They would remind people of the original covenant and God's decrees; call out specific instances of greed, idolatry, injustice, or unbelief; pronounce God's righteous judgment in line with his original covenant; and speak a message of comfort for the faithful.

One such prophet, named Elijah, was tasked with speaking these truths during the reign of a particularly evil king of Israel named Ahab, whose wife was the infamous Jezebel. As mentioned earlier, since the time of Joshua, the people had fallen into the worship of the Baals, or the agricultural gods of the land and people of Canaan. They would waver between Baal and Yahweh as the occasion dictated, fully serving neither one nor the other. This wavering was precisely what Elijah called out, demanding the people to choose whom they would serve. With mockery and sarcasm against Baal, Elijah demonstrated the full power of God. The display caused the Baal worshippers and bystanders to acknowledge that Yahweh was the true God. Elijah then killed the false prophets, the ones who had been vocally leading the people astray from Yahweh and into the worship of false gods. God's good covenant rightfully demanded everything of the people of Israel: their loyalty, their obedience, and their love. When kings and people continually turned away from him in idolatry, injustice, greed, and disobedience, God was not unfaithful to the covenant, and he brought curses upon them. Ultimately, as prophesied since Moses, the northern kingdom of Israel was conquered and exiled by the nation of Assyria in 722 BC, and it never fully reformed.

The southern kingdom of Judah also fell into sin and idolatry, but it was more of a slow fade. Their capital was still Jerusalem and their kings were still of the house and line of David. Again and again God proved his faithfulness in keeping a descendent of David on the throne, despite human attempts to the contrary. The southern kingdom of Judah watched the northern kingdom of Israel be led into captivity. Prophets continued to implore Judah to return to God and to not be like Israel, lest the same fate befall them as well. Some of the Davidic kings of the southern kingdom of Judah were godly, and their reforms prevented collapse at the same time as Israel. Eventually, however, the disobedience of the people was too much, and the southern kingdom was conquered, exiled, and led into captivity by the nation of Babylon in 586 BC.

Second Kings 25 records the fall of Jerusalem, the ultimate blow to the people. Their capital was invaded. The leaders were brutally tormented. The temple, the visible presence of God amid the people, was destroyed. The people were scattered and terrified. They had abandoned their God, and to the eyes of everyone it seemed that God had followed suit and abandoned them as well. But in the last verses of this chapter, we see a slim ray of hope. One aspect of the covenant was still standing: the king, the descendent of David, was allowed to live and was granted a fairly normal life even in exile. The covenant curses had indeed come upon the people of Israel and the people of Judah, but even amid destruction caused by their own disobedience, God was reminding them that he was still faithful to his covenant.

From the beginning until now, we have covered a major arc of the pattern of redemption. Creation and fall led to a calling of a people, captivity, exodus, covenant regulation, entry into and possession of the land, and the rule of David and the presence of the temple of Jerusalem. But since then, despite a few high points, this chapter of the story line of the Bible has been fairly disheartening. The people were called to unequivocal obedience, continued repentance, and unwavering loyalty to the God who had called and redeemed them. Again and again, however, they turned away from him and pursued other gods, and here at the end, the people are in exile and captivity just as they were in Egypt. It seemed like it was impossible for the people to keep the demands of the covenant, despite the faithfulness of God. Something had to change if the nation of Israel was to be all that God had called it to be.

Next week, we'll linger a bit longer in this doubt and uncertainty. We will see the mindset of the people as it seemed that all hope was lost. We'll see them cry out to God in confusion and despair. And we will see glimpses of what God will do next and how he will choose to continue his covenant, not abandoning his people but providing a new way for them. He will fulfill his promise that they will be his people and that he himself will be with them and be their God.

Days 16–20

Key Themes: As you go through the five days of study and the teaching section each week, look for the introduction or development of the following themes. These themes will build throughout the Old Testament (days 1–20) and will find their fulfillment in the New Testament (days 21–40), especially in the person and work of Jesus. New themes for the week will be in **bold**.

Creation	Redemption	David	**Shepherd**
Kingdom	Passover Lamb	Jerusalem	**Restoration**
Representative	Holiness (law)	Temple	**Israel**
Substitute	Priest		**Messiah**
"First Gospel"	Sacrifice		**Suffering Servant**
Covenant	King		**Glorious King**
Yahweh/Lord	Prophet		

16

Day

PSALM 89

Back in 2 Samuel 7 (see day 12), God had promised to establish the throne and dynasty of David forever. However, as we saw on day 15, due to the sin of the people, the kingdom was now in exile and hope was all but lost. One man, Ethan the Ezrahite, voiced a prayer on behalf of the nation both mourning the loss of the Davidic dynasty and pleading with God for its restoration in what we now call Psalm 89.

The prayer starts out celebrating God's love and faithfulness and praising him for making the covenant with David at all. The throne of Yahweh is characterized by "righteousness and justice" and "love and faithfulness" (v. 14), and those who walk with God "rejoice in [his] name all day long" (v. 16). The psalmist reiterates the amazing promises made to David—including the promises to discipline him (and by extension, his sons) when they do wrong—and confidently declares the glory of the covenant. "That his line will continue forever and his throne endure before me like the sun; it will be established forever like the moon, the faithful witness in the sky" (vv. 36–37). These exultant praises echo David's own prayer of amazed thanks at what God was graciously choosing to do for him and his family.

However, after a full thirty-seven verses of triumphant praise, the psalm abruptly shifts in tone and content. Now Ethan and the nation together cry out in confusion, "But you have rejected, you have spurned … you have renounced the covenant with your servant and have defiled his crown in the dust" (vv. 38–39). From their position in exile or on the brink of exile, these sentiments would have seemed like cruel reality. Surely God had abandoned them and had broken his covenant with David. They plead, "How long, O Lord?" (v. 46) and "Where is your former great love, which in your faithfulness you swore to David?" (v. 49).

Is this psalm contradicting itself? Is God faithful, or not? Does the covenant stand, or not? Are the people praising God, or accusing him of being far from them? Quite simply, this psalm is *honest*. The first part declares what they know to be true, even if they don't believe it, and the second part declares what seems to be true in the moment and what they are currently believing. How often are our prayers this honest? The psalmist declares the truth of God, but as the prayer goes on, we can see that his circumstances make this difficult and half-hearted. This does not stop him from crying out anyway. All throughout the psalms, a great hymnbook of human experience and emotion, we see echoes of this. For example, in Psalms 42 and 43, the same verse is repeated three times. "Why are you downcast, O my soul? Why so disturbed within me? Put your hope in God, for I will yet praise him, my Savior and my God" (42:5, 11; 43:5). It is almost as if the psalmist is preaching the truth to himself in the very midst of his pain-laden prayers. If God had in fact abandoned his covenant with David and with Israel, all hope was lost, and it certainly seemed that way right now. So the psalmist led the people in declaring truth *and* declaring their pain and confusion at the same time.

Notes

Read: Summarize what you read today. Write down any questions you have about the passage.

Reflect: What do you learn about God in these chapters, and/or what do you learn about people? How do these chapters contribute to the overall story line of the Bible? What key themes are introduced or developed here? (Refer to the list at the beginning of the week for help.)

Respond: Has God broken his covenant with David, or not? What truths do you need to declare to yourself amid pain and confusion? Are you being honest with yourself and with God about whatever you may be going through?

17

· Day ·

DANIEL 3

Many of the remaining books of the Old Testament, categorized loosely as the Prophets or Writings, tell the story of, or speak to, the exiles of the nation of Israel. They generally include a reminder or description of the sins of the people that led them to exile, hopeful reassurance that the Sovereign God is still in control, and anticipatory prophecy looking forward to a coming Messiah. Many familiar verses can be found in these books (for example, Jeremiah 29:11 and Isaiah 40:31), but those words of encouragement are most powerful when understood in their original context.

The people of Israel likely felt abandoned by their God. Here they were, in exile, torn away from familiarity and home and the good things that they had been given, due to their repeated and conscious breaking of the covenant they had made with God. It probably also seemed like God wasn't really in control; after all, enemy nations had been victorious over both Israel and Judah and led the people off into captivity. Surely Babylon's King Nebuchadnezzar was more powerful than the Lord. The exiles must have felt guilty, disappointed, and utterly hopeless.

Yet God had decidedly not abandoned them, and he was still very much in control. He was punishing them, yes, but not forever. In Jeremiah 29:4–7, the prophet gives a surprising injunction to the exiles on how they should use their time. "This is what the Lord Almighty, the God of Israel, says to all those I carried into exile from Jerusalem to Babylon: 'Build houses and settle down; plant gardens and eat what they produce. Marry and have sons and daughters … Seek the peace and prosperity of the city to which I have carried you into exile. Pray to the Lord for it, because it if prospers, you too will prosper.'" Although this is not what they would have chosen, they were to use this time well and seek their good and the good of the city—ultimately to the glory of God.

Several men who did this well were Belteshazzar (also known as Daniel), Shadrach, Meshach, and Abednego, who had been especially chosen by the Babylonian king Nebuchadnezzar because of their wisdom, knowledge, and dedication. They learned the ways of Babylon and became respected wise men and scholars. However, they never forgot their true God. Today's reading demonstrates their ultimate faith, as they chose to be thrown into the fire rather than denounce the name of their God.

The story might be familiar: the three friends refuse to bow down to the idol that the king has made, so they are thrown into the furnace, but they are saved by God and emerge without even the smell of smoke on their clothes. It is truly a miraculous and wonderful event that demonstrates the power of the Lord and his sovereignty over King Nebuchadnezzar and his golden statue.

But it is worth noting that verses 16–18 show that the three friends were not guaranteed this outcome when faced with the fiery furnace. They boldly assert to the king, "The God we serve is able to save us from it, and he will rescue us. *But even if he does not*, we want you to know, O King, that we will not serve your gods." They knew that their God was sovereign and powerful, even if he decided not to intervene on their behalf. Their faith was not based on miracles alone, nor did they only choose to follow God when times were easy. Rather, they trusted fully in the goodness and nature and utter sovereignty of the God of Israel, even amid a hopeless situation.

Notes

Read: Summarize what you read today. Write down any questions you have about the passage.

Reflect: What do you learn about God in these chapters, and/or what do you learn about people? How do these chapters contribute to the overall story line of the Bible? What key themes are introduced or developed here? (Refer to the list at the beginning of the week for help.)

Respond: When have you found yourself in a situation that seemed hopeless, whether through the actions of yourself or other people? Based on God's words to the exiles, how do you think that God would want you to live in that situation? What do you think about the three friends' assertion that even if God does not save them, he is still able and good and in control?

18

ISAIAH 9:1–7 AND ISAIAH 53 AND 61

Isaiah 9:1–7 brings us to a great and majestic prophecy pointing forward to the ultimate Savior of Judah: the promised Messiah. From the same land that is currently being invaded by a powerful enemy, a light will shine, and the instruments of war will be turned into instruments of peace (v. 5). And then, verse 6 reveals the means of this salvation: a child! But not just any child. This is no mere man. The government will rest upon his shoulders, he will reign on the throne of David, and he is the Wonderful Counselor, the Mighty God, the Everlasting Father, the Prince of Peace. God himself will come in the form of a child in order to save not only Judah but the entire human race and all of creation.

But there is a problem. How can a holy God come to dwell with sinful men and women? The rest of Isaiah 9 shifts abruptly in tone and outlines why God is allowing an enemy to invade his people. Quite simply, they are not following him. They have become prideful (v. 8–12), seeking the praise of great men (v. 13–17) and utterly lacking in brotherly love (v. 18–21). They refuse to acknowledge God, and they have turned away from him and gone their own way. Why should any Messiah come and dwell with these people? There seems to be no hope at all.

Enter **Isaiah 53**. There is hope, but it is not what they—or we—ever would have expected. This chapter is the last of four passages later in Isaiah that present a shocking, scandalous picture of this promised Messiah. He will not come first as a mighty warrior to rescue all the people of Israel from every enemy. Rather, he will come as a servant—and a suffering servant at that. He will be "despised and rejected by men, a man of sorrows, and acquainted with grief" (v. 3). He will be oppressed and afflicted, led to slaughter like a lamb, and his soul will make an offering for the guilt of others. This doesn't sound like a powerful Messiah. This doesn't sound like what was expected.

But it was all because of us. "All we like sheep have gone astray; we have turned—every one—to his own way; and the Lord has laid on him the iniquity of us all" (v. 6). And it was all for us. "But he was pierced for *our* transgressions; he was crushed for *our* iniquities; upon him was the chastisement that brought *us* peace, and with his wounds *we* are healed" (v. 5). How was this Wonderful Counselor, Mighty God, going to be able to dwell with sinful humans? By taking the punishment that we deserved upon himself. With *his* wounds, *we* are healed. This God so wanted reconciliation with his people—with Judah, with Israel, with me, and with you—that he would literally love us to death.

Seven hundred years after this prophecy was written, God would become a man in the person of Jesus of Nazareth. Jesus was despised and rejected, led to the cross like a lamb to the slaughter, in order that his wounds might heal his people. This passage is the most quoted Old Testament passage in the New Testament, and for good reason. It proclaims the glorious gospel seven centuries before Jesus walked the earth. His death was hardly the unfortunate circumstances of a political climate. It was the key to God's sovereign plan to redeem his people and bring his kingdom to earth.

Then **Isaiah 61** speaks of a year of the Lord's favor: a time when the warrior Messiah would come in the Spirit of God to bind up the brokenhearted, set prisoners free, and vanquish every enemy. When Jesus began his earthly ministry, he read part of this passage in the temple (Luke 4:18–19) and said, "Today this Scripture has been fulfilled in your hearing" (v. 21). He knew that he was the promised Messiah, sent from God to save his people from their sins. But before he would become the warrior Messiah, he would be the suffering servant, and the Lord would lay on him the iniquity of us all.

Notes

Read: Summarize what you read today. Write down any questions you have about the passage.

Reflect: What do you learn about God in these chapters, and/or what do you learn about people? How do these chapters contribute to the overall story line of the Bible? What key themes are introduced or developed here? (Refer to the list at the beginning of the week for help.)

Respond: What type of Messiah does Isaiah 9 set up, and how does that contrast with the Messiah set up in Isaiah 53? What are some common expectations about what a Messiah or Savior should be? This side of the cross, we can easily recognize Jesus in Isaiah 53. What parts of this chapter are most meaningful to you as you consider Jesus's death on your behalf?

19

Day

JEREMIAH 31

Jeremiah was another prophet who spoke to the people of Israel and Judah before and during the exile. Their own sins had caused their downfall, and God's righteous judgment is a significant theme of the book. However, he often speaks of a topic that may have seemed impossible at the time: restoration.

In this chapter, God first affirms his love for his people, even amid their own sin and rebellion. "I have loved you with an everlasting love; I have drawn you with loving-kindness" (v. 3). He then promises that they will not always experience hardship, pain, and discipline as they now are. Though righteous judgment must come, he promises, "I will build you up again … again you will take up your tambourines … again you will plant vineyards" (vv. 4–5). At the time of this writing, the people of Judah will soon be deported to Babylon; their enemy is even now at the gate. Yet God declares that they will come back!

Then we come to the highest point of Jeremiah's prophecy and the glorious affirmation that Yahweh is still at work. The Lord, the covenant God of Abraham, Isaac, Jacob, Moses, and David, will make a "new covenant" with Israel. "'I will put my law in their minds and write it on their hearts. I will be their God, and they will be my people. No longer will a man teach his neighbor, or a man his brother, saying, "Know the Lord," because they will all know me, from the least of them to the greatest,' declares the Lord. 'For I will forgive their wickedness and remember their sins no more'" (vv. 33–34). Instead of tablets of stone, this covenant would be written on the tablets of human hearts. People wouldn't need to rely on special teachers, for personal and intimate knowledge of God would be accessible to everyone. And the main problem with the old covenants, namely, the people's sin, would be definitely dealt with once and for all. This covenant, like the old ones, would be enacted by the shedding of blood, but this would be a different blood altogether from the blood of bulls and goats.

This new covenant promises internal change to a people who would soon experience utter ruin. They must have clung to these words as they were led away from their homeland. When they returned, as promised, seventy years later, they must have wondered if this new covenant would come to pass anytime soon. Four hundred years would go by before a baby's cry in the city of David would indicate that the mediator of this new covenant had come at last. And when Jesus clearly declared, "This cup is the new covenant in my blood, which is poured out for you" (Luke 22:20), the new covenant was put into effect once and for all.

Notes

Read: Summarize what you read today. Write down any questions you have about the passage.

Reflect: What do you learn about God in these chapters, and/or what do you learn about people? How do these chapters contribute to the overall story line of the Bible? What key themes are introduced or developed here? (Refer to the list at the beginning of the week for help.)

Respond: How is this new covenant similar to the old covenants we have seen? How is it different? The phrase "new covenant" here is later translated as "New Testament," what we today call the distinctly Christian part of the Bible. How is this promise of a new covenant significant in the lives of believers today?

20

EZRA 3

The people of Judah remained in exile in Babylon for approximately seventy years. But when the Babylonian kingdom was itself taken over by the kingdom of the Medes and the Persians, the Persian king Cyrus allowed the exiles to return to their homeland, to the place that God had promised to Abraham, Isaac, and Jacob so many years before. They had to start over, rebuilding everything that had been burned down or taken from them. It is difficult to imagine the myriad emotions and thoughts that these captives of war experienced upon returning home. Doubtless they were thrilled to be back, but it was likely a quiet excitement mixed with sadness and grief for all that had occurred in the meantime.

When the Babylonian army had besieged Jerusalem decades earlier, one of the things they destroyed and plundered was Solomon's temple. As we have seen, the temple was the house of God, the focal point of their worship, and the representation of God's presence among them, so its destruction was felt deeply. Almost immediately upon their return from exile, the people set out to rebuild the temple. It was no match for the grandeur of Solomon's temple. In fact, people old enough to remember the original wept because the new one simply didn't compare (verse 12). But it was also a sign of redemption and restoration, and people praised the goodness of God for bringing them back.

The rebuilding of this temple marks the end of the historical narrative of the Old Testament. The people of Israel had been told that a Messiah was coming, that their kingdom would be restored, and they looked forward to the day when a powerful king would rise up and bring justice against all of their enemies. But for about four hundred years, God was quiet, and all they could do was wait and hope. True, heart-level redemption and restoration were still needed. The people were clearly unable to accomplish this on their own, and they failed again and again. The only solution would be for God himself to make a way.

Notes

Read: Summarize what you read today. Write down any questions you have about the passage.

Reflect: What do you learn about God in these chapters, and/or what do you learn about people? How do these chapters contribute to the overall story line of the Bible? What key themes are introduced or developed here? (Refer to the list at the beginning of the week for help.)

Respond: The first twenty days of this overview of the Bible have traced the historical narrative of the Old Testament. What has been new to you? Confusing? Surprising? Do you feel like you have a better understanding of the story line of the Bible thus far and how it sets up the coming of Jesus?

Days 16–20: Summary and Teaching

We are now halfway through our forty-day overview of the Bible and the story line of how God is working out his grand plan of redemption. Last week, we saw that Yahweh, the covenant God of the people of Israel, maintained his faithfulness to his covenants with Abraham, Isaac, Jacob, and Moses by bringing them into a good land with a good king in David. He then made another astonishing covenant with David in which he promised to make his house and his lineage endure forever, with a descendant of David eternally on the throne. Throughout the next generations, the kingdom was divided, and the northern kingdom of Israel fell to captivity under Assyria. Even though the southern kingdom of Judah maintained a descendant of David on the throne, and even though prophets warned them again and again to turn back to the Lord, the sins of the people caught up with them. And again, in keeping with God's covenant, the southern kingdom was also exiled into captivity by the nation of Babylon in 586 BC.

We picked up this week in a place of disappointment, despair, and confusion. Without a doubt, the people's sin was responsible for their current situation. God had called them to be a light to the world, but their continued and unrepentant greed, idolatry, injustice, and unrighteousness clearly showed how far they had fallen. They had presumed upon the grace of God, taking for granted that the blessings would always be there, no matter what they did. Had they fallen too far? Did they miss their chance? What hope was there to live in relationship with a holy God if they could not keep the commandments written on tablets of stone?

Psalm 89 saw the writer in mourning for the downfall of the Davidic kingdom, pleading for its restoration. Daniel 3 gave us a picture of a few exiles who were still faithful to their covenant God. Isaiah and Jeremiah explained that something better was coming and that not all hope was lost. And finally, Ezra 3 saw the return of the exiles to their own land after seventy long years, but it is ultimately a disappointment and a reminder that something better was needed. Let's dive in and see how God has been at work through this time, even in the middle of incredibly difficult circumstances.

One of the many beautiful things about the book of Psalms is that we see an incredible range of honest emotions as the writers reflect their experiences back to God. Here in Psalm 89, the psalmist initially praises God for his might, for his awesomeness, for his wonders, and for his covenant with David. But then the psalm shifts abruptly—as abruptly as the experience must have been. God seemed incredibly distant. Had he broken his covenant? Would he prove to be a disappointment after all? The psalmist must have echoed the thoughts of the nation. Was it over? Would God redeem his people again? And if so, how long would it be until then?

As we grapple with these questions, let us also remember that these things weren't new. Moses had warned about sin, judgment, and restoration way back in Deuteronomy 4:23–31.

> Be careful not to forget the covenant of the Lord your God that he made with you; do not make for yourselves an idol in the form of anything the Lord your God has forbidden. For the Lord your God is a consuming fire, a jealous God. After you have had children and grandchildren and have lived in the land a long time—if you then become corrupt and make any kind of idol, doing evil in the eyes of the Lord your God and arousing his anger, I call the heavens and the earth as witnesses against you this day that you will quickly perish from the land that you are crossing the Jordan to possess. You will not live there long but will certainly be destroyed. The Lord will scatter you among the peoples, and only a few of you will survive among the nations to which the Lord will drive you. There you will worship man-made gods of wood and stone, which cannot see or hear or eat or smell. But if from there you seek the Lord your God, you will find him if you seek him with all your heart and with all your soul. When you are in distress and all these things have happened to you, then in later days you will return to the Lord your God and obey him. For the Lord your God is a merciful God; he will not abandon or destroy you or forget the covenant with your ancestors, which he confirmed to them by oath.

In this, we see again how God's *unconditional* conditional covenant plays itself out and how from the beginning God called his people not just out of captivity but into a new life, to be a royal priesthood and a holy nation in order to draw others to him.

It is worth comparing this God to the seemingly more benign God of the New Testament. John is known as the apostle who writes about love, with familiar sayings such as "Let us love one another, for love comes from God" (1 John 4:7). In the five short chapters of 1 John, he uses the word "love" *forty-four times.* But he also writes, "We know that we have come to know him if we obey his commands. The man who says, 'I know him' but does not do what he commands is a liar, and the truth is not in him. But if anyone obeys his word, God's love is truly made complete in him. This is how we know we are in him: Whoever claims to live in him must walk as Jesus did" (1 John 2:3–6). Just like in the Old Testament, love is the foundation and purpose of the covenant. Just like in the Old Testament, obedience is the result of the covenant. Just like in the Old Testament, redemption is by grace alone, but the resulting life needs to be, and will be, characterized by obedience. So here in Psalm 89, we see tremendous honesty as the writer praises God for his eternal sovereignty and awesomeness while also mourning the downfall of the nation, wondering what is going to happen next.

Another group of people who must have been wondering, "What now?" were the exiles themselves. They were away from their land, away from their temple, and away from everything they once knew. They were there as a result of the nation's sin, yes, but that didn't make the circumstances any easier. Many of the exiles continued to try to live in faithfulness to God, and several of the prophetic books, especially Ezekiel, are written specifically to the exiles, offering a message of comfort and a promise of revival and restoration. Most famous among these exiles in Babylon were the prophet Daniel, who shut the mouths of the lions and interpreted dreams, and his friends Shadrach, Meshach, and Abednego, who escaped unharmed from the fiery furnace.

Undoubtedly, these familiar stories inspire readers to stand up for their faith even amid harsh circumstances. But here, as with every place in the Bible, the full context of scripture makes it even richer. The psalmist had just expressed in heartbreaking poetry the disappointment that everyone must have felt with God. So even amid perceived abandonment and a reality that was so far from the Promised Land of their forefathers, these three men refused to serve any god beside Yahweh. Their response to King Nebuchadnezzar echoed their reality. "The God we serve is *able* to save us … but even if he does not, we want you to know, O King, that we will not serve your gods" (Daniel 3:17–18). Likewise, they knew that the God they served was *able* to deliver them immediately from their confusion, heartbreak, disappointment, guilt, and exile. But *even if he did not*, they were prepared to continue to serve him only.

They trusted in him, and he did not disappoint. While for Shadrach, Meshach, and Abednego God's faithfulness was immediately, and even bodily, apparent, this reality stood true for all of Israel: the people could continue to trust God, and they would not be put to shame. They would not ultimately be disappointed in the one who had called and redeemed them, even if they couldn't quite see what he was doing at the moment.

The prophets who spoke to the people of Israel and the people of Judah before, during, and after the exile began to speak also of one who would come, who would bring victory and peace for the nation and judgment and wrath for the oppressive and corrupt nations around them. This one who would come was called the Messiah, which means "Anointed One," echoing the anointings of priests and kings throughout the Old Testament.

In the Isaiah passages, we saw different portrayals of this one Messiah, some of which would have been rather startling to the original hearers. Isaiah 9 reveals that a child would be born—but not just any child. This child is equated with God himself. The titles applied to this coming one are stretched far beyond any human and are glorious in scope: Wonderful Counselor, Mighty God, Everlasting Father, and Prince of Peace. Isaiah 53 reveals that this one who would come would also suffer on behalf of the transgressions of others. Later, Isaiah 61 will reveal that there will be complete and total restoration of all things—not only physical and emotional healings but also large-scale justice for all of those currently in disgrace and shame.

It is easy for us to read Jesus into these passages, particularly into Isaiah 53. But keep in mind that these were written five hundred years before Jesus, to a specific people in a specific situation.

The acorn here is that a Messiah would come. There was hope. God was still in the covenant. He had not abandoned them. But who would this be? And when? Since the people of Israel were under almost constant oppression and subjugation, the people were probably most looking forward to the Isaiah 61 aspect of the Messiah. The others seemed so strange and obscure that it's no surprise that they thought maybe there would be multiple Messiahs.

Even when the oak revealed this multifaceted Messiah to be Jesus Christ, the people didn't understand. In Luke 4:17–21, Jesus stood up to read in the synagogue. "The scroll of the prophet Isaiah was handed to him. Unrolling it, he found the place where it is written: 'The Spirit of the Lord is on me, because he has anointed me to preach good news to the poor. He has sent me to proclaim freedom for the prisoners and recovery of sight for the blind, to release the oppressed, to proclaim the year of the Lord's favor.' Then he rolled up the scroll, gave it back to the attendant and sat down. The eyes of everyone in the synagogue were fastened on him, and he began by saying to them, 'Today this Scripture is fulfilled in your hearing.'" There is no question that he was applying this to himself, but he conveniently stopped reading and sat down halfway through the passage.

Similarly, in Luke 7:2–6, John the Baptist was imprisoned for his testimony about Jesus. He wasn't expecting this, based on how he had read this Isaiah passage, and it caused great doubt. He sent a messenger to ask Jesus, "Are you the one who was to come, or should we expect someone else?" Jesus replied with the same message as in the synagogue. The blind were receiving their sight, the dead were being raised, and the good news was being preached to the poor. This needed to be a sufficient answer to answer John's question of who Jesus was, but Jesus didn't immediately come and release him from prison. Once again, even John the Baptist had a different Messiah in mind, one who would immediately bring political revolution for Israel.

And in Matthew 16:21–23, Jesus is explaining to his disciples that he must suffer and die before being raised to life again. Peter pulls him aside and rebukes him, saying, "Never, Lord! This shall never happen to you." Jesus responds, "Get behind me, Satan! You do not have in mind the things of God, but the things of men." Even Jesus's closest friends and followers continued to have in mind the "things of men" and could not find a way to put these familiar passages together.

On this side of the cross, our own oak is still not fully formed, as we live in this already-but-not-yet tension. We saw that as in Isaiah 9, a child was born, and he is our Wonderful Counselor and the Mighty God, the Prince of Peace who was able to reconcile us to God. We see his death and resurrection played out in Isaiah 53. And we have seen glimpses of the glorious restoration and complete healing of Isaiah 61—but not the full picture. Not yet anyway.

Finally, Jeremiah 31, and the chapters that surround it, comprise one of the most hopeful sections of the entire Old Testament. The idea of a "new covenant" is spoken of again and again throughout the prophets, but Jeremiah presents it most clearly here. Yes, the people were currently under judgment. But passages like these reminded them that judgment was for discipline, and the entire purpose of discipline is for restoration. In light of this, the prophets envisioned restoration of relationship with God (a new covenant), God's promise for a coming day of the Lord, and a growing realization of the coming King. As mentioned earlier, the people knew of a coming Messiah, or Anointed One. Throughout the prophets, he is referred to in different places as a prophet, a priest, a shepherd, and a king. It would be impossible for one person to fill all of these offices under the Old Covenant. But here in Jeremiah, we clearly see the idea of a New Covenant.

> "The time is coming," declares the Lord, "when I will make a new covenant with the house of Israel and with the house of Judah. It will not be like the covenant I made with their forefathers when I took them by the hand to lead them out of Egypt, because they broke my covenant, though I was a husband to them," declares the Lord. "This is the covenant I will make with the house of Israel after that time," declares the Lord. "I will put my law in their minds and write it on their hearts. I will be their God, and they will be my people. No longer will a man teach his neighbor, or a man his brother, saying, 'Know the Lord,' because they will all know me, from the least of them to the greatest," declares the Lord. "For I will forgive their wickedness and remember their sins no more." (Jeremiah 31:31–34)

A new covenant! Does this nullify the old ones? Are the covenants we have seen—the ones with Abraham, Moses, and David—now invalid or void? There are a few similarities and dissimilarities to point out here.

First, it is worth remembering that at no point is any fault laid upon the old covenants themselves—not the Abrahamic, Mosaic, or Davidic. More than that, the language is much the same, and the repetition of "declares the Lord" is significant since that Lord is Yahweh, the name of the covenant God of Israel. Even by using that name, he is linking himself to what has come before.

The fault was with the people. The idea of this new covenant being "written on their hearts" as opposed to written on tablets of stone may suggest that this covenant is meant to be internal, while the old ones were merely external. However, many verses throughout the Old Testament—especially the entire book of Deuteronomy—stress that the goal of the covenants has *always* been internalization, a true love for God. When Jesus states the greatest commandments as loving God and loving your neighbor, he is taking these directly from the law. In fact, one of the main causes of judgment was that Israel had divorced the internal from the external, continuing their religious activity with hearts far from God.

The entire reason that the people were not able to keep the old covenants was because of sin. Their continued rebellion against God, their infidelity to the covenant, and their inability to walk in the ways of holiness all came down to their sin. In his great mercy, God provided ways for their sin to be dealt with. The system of law, priests, and sacrifices—while it may seem odd or overwhelming to us—was meant, from the beginning, to allow a sinful people to dwell with a holy God. Forgiveness of sins was based on the shedding of the blood of animals, but both the sacrifices and the priests offering the sacrifices were imperfect, and therefore the acts had to be repeated again and again. Here in the new covenant though, sin has been dealt with finally and definitively.

Additionally, although this is a covenant, there is no part for Israel as there has been in the past. God says, "*I* will put my law in their minds and hearts. *I* will be their God. *I* will forgive their wickedness." Even the grammar of this passage points to the role of Yahweh. Instead of just "I will put my law in their minds and hearts," because of the repetition and emphasis of the subject, it really says, "*I* will put my law in their minds and hearts. *I* will be their God. *I* will forgive their wickedness and will remember their sins no more."

Looking ahead to next week, what is ultimately new in the new covenant is Jesus. He will be the Messiah, the perfect king, the perfect priest, the perfect sacrifice, the perfect prophet, and the perfect shepherd. He will come to his own, but his own will not receive him. But to those who do receive him, he will give the right to become children of God (see John 1:11–12). And through his death and resurrection, he will open the way for this reality of a New Covenant.

At last, after seventy years in exile, a new regional superpower emerged, and the Persian king Cyrus sent the Jewish people back to their own land. And here, the narrative of the Old Testament ends—with nothing fully resolved. The people were scattered and beaten down, but this was the best-case scenario. The exiles had returned home and were able to rebuild the altar and the temple, visible manifestations of the presence of God. Yet we saw in this chapter that those who had seen the former temple wept at the sight of the new one, which paled in comparison. It was a joyful time as well, and "no one could distinguish the sound of the shouts of joy from the sound of weeping" (Ezra 13). The people knew that they had sinned and that God's judgment had come upon them as he had promised from long ago. Even the best of reparations couldn't bring them back to the heights from which they had fallen. God was still with them; he had remained and would continue to remain faithful to his covenant. The problem was not with the covenant or with God. The problem was with the people. And for four hundred years, these people waited to see what their God would do next.

This week marks the halfway point of this study and the last time we will be in the Old Testament. Through the last four weeks, we have seen God create the world and human beings mess up the world. For no reason other than his love for his people, we have seen God make covenants with Abraham, Moses, and David. Each had its own specifics, but in all of them, he promised to dwell with his people, to be their God, to multiply them and make their name great for the sake of the world, and to establish the line of David as a kingship forever.

Again and again, God has proved faithful to his covenants. But again and again, the people proved unfaithful. Finally, their idolatry and rebellion led to their exile from the Promised Land. When they returned seventy years later, hope seemed all but lost. This week, we saw an honest psalm cry out with confusion as to where God's promises were now. We saw three faithful exiles who admitted that God might not show up in the way they wanted, but they would follow him nonetheless. And we saw a promise of God that someday a child would be born who would change everything. He reminded them that he loved them with an everlasting love, and he explained that a new covenant was on the way. Finally, we saw a portion of Israel return to their homeland. They were able to rebuild part of their lives and their temple, but it was clear that things would never truly return to the way they had been. So they awaited the coming of this glorious Messiah.

And next week, we will see every one of God's promises come true.

Days 21–25

Key Themes: Now that these themes have been developed in the Old Testament, take note of how they are continued or fulfilled in the New Testament.

Creation	Redemption	David	Shepherd
Kingdom	Passover Lamb	Jerusalem	Restoration
Representative	Holiness (law)	Temple	Israel
Substitute	Priest		Messiah
"First Gospel"	Sacrifice		Suffering Servant
Covenant	King		Glorious King
Yahweh/Lord	Prophet		

21
Day

LUKE 1–2

After hundreds of years of apparent silence from God, the birth of two baby boys was foretold by angels. The first pronouncement was to an old, barren couple who would give birth to John the Baptist. His ministry would pave the way for Jesus. "Many of the people of Israel will he bring back to the Lord their God" (1:16). The second pronouncement was to a skeptical young virgin who, by the power of the Holy Spirit, would give birth to the long-awaited Messiah.

The angel's announcement to Mary was one of tremendous significance. "He will be great and will be called the Son of the Most High. The Lord God will give him the throne of his father David, and he will reign over the house of Jacob forever; his kingdom will never end" (1:32–33). Many of the themes and promises that we saw throughout the Old Testament are fulfilled here. Not only would he be the promised Messiah, but he would also be the Son of God himself. Furthermore, he would ascend to the throne once promised to David (2 Samuel 7:13, 16; see reading from day 12) and would reign forevermore (Isaiah 9:6–7; see reading from day 19). Even Zechariah's song picks up on the promises to both Abraham and David.

This wonderful and miraculous Christmas story is rightly precious to us. But it goes so much deeper than children in bathrobes at pageants or Nativity scenes on mantles. This was what the people had been waiting for. This was God's answer to the problem of sin begun all the way back in Genesis 3. This was the fulfillment of everything that had come before. Later, the apostle Paul would put it this way: "But when the time had fully come, God sent his Son, born of a woman, born under law, to redeem those under law, that we might receive the full rights of sons" (Galatians 4:4–5).

So as shepherds sang in the fields and kings traveled from the east, we know that all of heaven joined with Mary, Joseph, Elizabeth, and Zechariah in rejoicing that *it was time*. The redemption of Israel, and of all of humanity, had begun.

Notes

Read: Summarize what you read today. Write down any questions you have about the passage.

Reflect: What do you learn about God in these chapters, and/or what do you learn about people? How do these chapters contribute to the overall story line of the Bible? What key themes are developed or fulfilled here? (Refer to the list at the beginning of the week for help.)

Respond: How does the Christmas story have new meaning for you after the readings in the Old Testament? What themes, types, or prophecies in the Old Testament did the birth of Jesus fulfill? What elements of this familiar story are most precious to you, and why?

22

Day

JOHN 1:1–18

The first words of today's reading, "In the beginning," take the reader back to Genesis 1 (see reading for day 1) and to the account of creation. Way back then, this "Word" was *with* God and *was* God. He was both distinct from him and of the same essence as him. What we read in English as "Word" comes from the Greek word *logos*. This is God's logic, his reason, the spoken word that brought forth creation and revelation. A word reveals, discloses, and uncovers what previously could not fully be understood. A person can have many thoughts in his head and others might know some of them through actions or expressions, but until he forms words, the thoughts cannot be truly known by anyone else. Same with God. He had revealed himself in many ways in the Old Testament, but this Word finally made him completely known and knowable.

So who or what is this Word? It is more than just God's speaking into creation. Instead, verse 14 explains that "the Word became flesh and dwelt among us." This Word is Jesus. Jesus became man in order to narrate the invisible God and to make him known. The One through whom all things were made (v. 3) put on human flesh and walked among us. As we have seen in the Old Testament, before Solomon built the temple, the place where God would dwell with his people was called the tabernacle. The priests would make sacrifices in the tabernacle, and the people saw it as a holy place. Here the original text says that Jesus "tabernacled" among us. This person of Jesus became for us the means through which God would dwell with his people.

Again, in verse 18, John makes this clear. "No one has ever seen God; the only God, who is at the Father's side, he has made him known." Jesus revealed to us in relatable, human form what previously could not truly be understood. In the words of theologian D. A. Carson, John 1:18 "summarizes how the 'Word' which was with God in the very beginning came into the sphere of time, history, tangibility—in other words, how the Son of God was sent into the world to become the Jesus of history, so that the glory and grace of God might be uniquely and perfectly disclosed."[5]

Consider for a moment how far the Almighty God has gone in pursuit of us. Though he was completely holy, immortal, untouchable, and completely set apart, *God became man.* He became one of us. He walked among us in this broken, messed-up world. In the person of Jesus, we could touch God, listen to God, and see God face-to-face. If he has gone so far, can he not be trusted with what we are going through today? He is not distant. He is near. As we read about the life, death, and resurrection of Jesus over the next few days, let us keep in mind that this person of Jesus was not just a nice person or a good teacher. He was God himself who came to dwell with us.

Finally, look at verses 11–12. Even after all this, his people did not receive him, and he was "despised and rejected" (Isaiah 53:3; see reading for day 18). But for all who did receive him, both then and now, he gave the right to become children of God!

---

[5] D. A. Carson, *The Gospel according to John*, The Pillar New Testament Commentary (APOLLOS: Leicester, 1991), 111.

Notes

Read: Summarize what you read today. Write down any questions you have about the passage.

Reflect: What do you learn about God in these chapters, and/or what do you learn about people? How do these chapters contribute to the overall story line of the Bible? What key themes are developed or fulfilled here? (Refer to the list at the beginning of the week for help.)

Respond: Whereas yesterday's reading communicated the birth of Jesus in a historical narrative way, today's reading communicates it in a more theological way. How do the two passages complement and enhance one another? Why is it significant that Jesus is called the "Word" of God? Have you received him and believed in his name?

23
Day

LUKE 4

Before Jesus began his earthly ministry, he was tempted by the devil to take shortcuts. Both of them knew that Jesus had a long and painful road ahead of him, and Satan offered him world domination without the suffering. This may have been a reasonable offer; elsewhere, Satan is called "the prince of this world" (John 12:31), "the god of this age" (2 Corinthians 4:4), and "the ruler of the kingdom of the air" (Ephesians 2:2). He tested Jesus, tempted him, and quoted scripture to try to back up his claims.

But that suffering was precisely why Jesus came in the first place, and Jesus responded strongly by also quoting scripture—but in the right way. This temptation occurred after forty days of fasting in the desert, and Jesus would have been in an incredibly weak state. However, he never lost sight of the mission that his Father had called him to, and he would not take shortcuts to get there, no matter how attractive they may have seemed at the moment. The author of Hebrews would later write that "we do not have a high priest [Jesus] who is unable to sympathize with our weaknesses, but we have one who has been tempted in every way, just as we are—yet was without sin" (Hebrews 4:15). We can therefore call on him with confidence to receive mercy and grace, because we know that he has been there too.

The rest of the chapter describes the beginnings of Jesus's activity during his ministry. He spoke in the synagogue to mixed results (compare v. 22 to vv. 28–30), yet he never stopped proclaiming the truth of who he was. He used the Old Testament scriptures to point out to the people that he was, in fact, the promised Messiah (see reading for day 18). He drove out evil spirits and healed the sick. He began to do for the people *physically* what his ultimate work would accomplish for us *spiritually*. His name and his work began to spread across the region, and wherever he went he repeated, "I must preach the good news of the kingdom of God to the other towns also, because that is why I was sent" (v. 43). Though the people had varying reactions, this good news—this *gospel*—began to work its way into the hearts and lives of all who heard it.

Notes

Read: Summarize what you read today. Write down any questions you have about the passage.

Reflect: What do you learn about God in these chapters, and/or what do you learn about people? How do these chapters contribute to the overall story line of the Bible? What key themes are developed or fulfilled here? (Refer to the list at the beginning of the week for help.)

Respond: How can we use scripture to fight off temptation, as Jesus did? How does this passage set up Jesus's role as high priest on our behalf? In what ways does Jesus fulfill the scripture that he himself read?

24
Day

MATTHEW 5–7

Today's passage is known as the Sermon on the Mount. In the book of Matthew, it is Jesus's first public discourse, and it summarizes his teachings about how the people of God should live. Note how many times Jesus says, "You have heard it said ... but I say to you ..." regarding various commandments and laws. It might seem as if Jesus is completely doing away with the laws and customs of the Old Testament; indeed, Christians today no longer practice many of the culturally specific laws of the nation of Israel. However, Jesus clarifies that he "did not come to abolish [the law and the prophets] but to fulfill them" (5:17).

Many teachers of the Old Testament law would add rules upon rules, all with specific exceptions, which ultimately distorted the original purpose of God's good law and allowed for injustice to creep in. But here, with each scenario that he presents—murder, adultery, and divorce—Jesus takes the original law and moves it to an internal, heart-level issue.

These new commands are much more difficult. Some of them might even seem impossible. Love your enemies, do not look at another lustfully, seek the kingdom of God first, and do not worry—much of this seems out of our control. And that's precisely the point. The external rules and regulations do not transform our hearts and are therefore not sufficient to save. But even in the Old Testament, God had promised, "I will give you a new heart and put a new spirit in you; I will remove from you your heart of stone and give you a heart of flesh. And I will put my Spirit in you and move you to follow my decrees and be careful to keep all of my laws" (Ezekiel 36:26–27). This was why Jesus came. We needed to be transformed from the inside out. We needed to be born again.

Notes

Read: Summarize what you read today. Write down any questions you have about the passage.

Reflect: What do you learn about God in these chapters, and/or what do you learn about people? How do these chapters contribute to the overall story line of the Bible? What key themes are developed or fulfilled here? (Refer to the list at the beginning of the week for help.)

Respond: Of all the various issues covered in the Sermon on the Mount, which one speaks to you most today, and why? What do you find challenging or even impossible? This passage serves as King Jesus's inaugural address. With this in mind, what should the lives of the citizens of the kingdom of heaven look like?

25

JOHN 3

Yesterday's reading pointed us to the fact that we need a new heart. Similarly, today's reading finds Jesus explaining that we need to be born again. Nicodemus, this Pharisee (Jewish teacher of the law), is rightly confused. He assumes that Jesus is speaking of another physical birth, but Jesus explains to him that it is a spiritual rebirth. Because of the sin of Adam and Eve (see reading for day 2), each of us is born with our hearts bent toward sin and rebellion against God. We need a fresh start, a clean slate before God. We need a total and complete salvation.

Jesus goes on to assert that this salvation is in him. "For God so loved the world that he gave his one and only Son, that whoever believes in him shall not perish but have eternal life. For God did not send his Son into the world to condemn the world, but to save the world through him" (vv. 16–17). These familiar verses are full of precious promises. God loved us *so much* that he would send his Son to die on our behalf, and as a result, we can have eternal life in him! Throughout the Old Testament, we saw the people of God trying and failing to live up to the standard of holiness that would allow sinful people to reside with him. Even here, in this passage, we see that people reject Jesus and his message because they love their darkness and their sin (v. 19). But here too, we see that for those who believe, God himself has provided the way. In our new birth and with our new heart that God has graciously offered, we are now changed from the inside out to love God more than we love our darkness.

Notes

Read: Summarize what you read today. Write down any questions you have about the passage.

Reflect: What do you learn about God in these chapters, and/or what do you learn about people? How do these chapters contribute to the overall story line of the Bible? What key themes are developed or fulfilled here? (Refer to the list at the beginning of the week for help.)

Respond: What do you think Jesus meant by saying, "You must be born again"? Comparing this to a physical birth, what implications does this have for our spiritual rebirth? How does John 3:16 sum up the gospel message?

Days 21–25: Summary and Teaching

In the first half of our study, we read through key chapters in the Old Testament and discussed how God was establishing covenants, norms, and types with the people of Israel. We saw how Yahweh, the covenant God of Abraham, Isaac, and Jacob, remained faithful to his promises. We saw his pattern of redemption for the world. After he created everything good, men and women rebelled against his kingdom and his perfect rule. But he brought his people out of slavery, gave them instructions for holy living, and established them in a community and in a good land. Eventually, however, the people forgot God and his covenants with them. Due to their sinful natures and deeds, they were unable to keep the covenants. In his great mercy, God instituted a system of priests, kings, sacrifices, and prophets to serve as mediators, but God's righteous judgment ultimately came in the form of a seventy-year exile in the land of Babylon. Their city was razed, the temple was destroyed, and the people were either killed or transported. This was the lowest point for the nation of Israel in the Old Testament. After they returned home, the exiles were left wondering what would happen next. When would a promised Messiah-King come? Would he immediately bring political freedom and revolution to the embittered nation as the prophets seemed to suggest?

This week, as we entered the New Testament—or New Covenant—we can start to see how every single one of God's promises was fulfilled in Jesus. The time had come for the Messiah to be born, but there were parts of his coming that were so unexpected that even faithful believers missed who he was. Luke 1–2 documented the long-awaited birth of Jesus, while John 1:1–18 clarified who exactly this Jesus was. Luke 4 showed us how Jesus was the *true* Adam and the *true* Israel as he overcame the temptations that they had succumbed to. Matthew 5–7 showed how Jesus both fulfilled and internalized the law. And John 3 revealed God's plan for the world.

As we dig deeper into these chapters, keep in mind that as the New Testament unfolds the story of Jesus, he is fulfilling all the expectations of the Old Testament. The New Testament gospel and terminology are grounded in the preparatory shadows of the Old. Our word "Christ" means "Messiah" or "Anointed One"; allow what you have learned from the Old Testament to deepen your understanding of what it means for Jesus to be the Christ.

Before we even meet Jesus or his parents, we meet Zechariah and Elizabeth: two old, barren, faithful Israelites who are miraculously promised a son. The boy, who would come to be known as John the Baptist, would prepare the way for Jesus as one last prophet. He too has links to the Old Testament. Luke 1:17 says that "he will go on before the Lord, in the spirit and power of Elijah" in order to prepare the people for the person, words, and work of Jesus. He wasn't Elijah resurrected, but his message and his purpose would be the same as what we saw when Elijah confronted the prophets of Baal on Mount Carmel (see day 14): repent, turn to God, serve him only, and listen to the message he has for you. Not only this, but Elizabeth and Mary, who were relatives, were able to encourage one another as they prepared for their unique, miraculous births.

Then the angel Gabriel comes on the scene. We are immediately told two things about Mary. She was a virgin, and she was engaged to be married to a descendent of David. This child was a true miracle from the beginning, one born of the Holy Spirit. From conception, he was fully God and fully man, able to be a perfect human and live a sinless life. Then, although he would not be Joseph's biological son, this child would be the heir of Joseph once he and Mary were married and therefore a descendant of David. This is of *enormous* significance, given the promises made to David and his family back in 2 Samuel 7 (see day 12)! Remember that God had told him that he would establish his throne *forever*, a promise that even initially seemed to stretch beyond normal human imaginings. Through exile and faithlessness, God had maintained his promises to the house of David in the Old Testament, and here we see their ultimate fulfillment. The angel Gabriel, speaking to Mary, explicitly states this connection in verses 32–33. "The Lord God will give him the throne of his father David, and he will reign over the house of Jacob forever; his kingdom will never end."

Additionally, the angel declares that his name is to be Jesus. That name is the Greek form of the name Joshua, which means "the Lord saves"—and the Lord is Yahweh, the covenant God of Israel. This baby will function as a second Joshua, leading his people into the *true* Promised Land, and the connection with the old covenants is already clear from the name. We are only thirty-three verses into one of the New Testament gospels, and already we are seeing how Jesus is fulfilling all of the promises made in the Old.

When Mary praises God in her hymn that has come to be known as the Magnificat, she undoubtedly understood at least *some* of the significance of the child she was carrying. And when Zechariah equally praised God when his son John was born, he sums up the truth nicely through the Holy Spirit about both his son and about Mary's son. "Praise be to the Lord, the God of Israel, because he has come and has redeemed his people. He has raised up a horn of salvation for us in the house of his servant David (as he said through his holy prophets long ago) … to show mercy to our fathers and to remember his holy covenant, the oath he swore to our father Abraham" (vv. 68–73). Jesus hasn't even been born yet, and already the people involved can see the link between the preparatory shadows and covenants of the Old Testament and what is about to happen.

Then in Luke 2, by God's providence, due to a census far out of Joseph's control, Jesus ends up being born in Bethlehem, the city of David. The angels proclaimed it to the shepherds, of all people. "Today in the city of David a Savior has been born to you; he is Christ the Lord" (2:11). This was the one they had been waiting for! And when he brought to earth "peace to men on whom his favor rests," it was far deeper than the Pax Romana of their current Roman world. This was eternal peace with God, echoing back to Isaiah 9's title of "Prince of Peace." This would not be an immediate tranquility for all people though, since peace with God means opposition to the powers of the world: the flesh and the devil. But this baby Jesus had come to save the people from their sins. Even lying in that manger, he was the Son of God.

The rest of Luke 2 shows us how devout Joseph and Mary were in keeping the law of Moses for both postbirth purification and for observing the Passover. Even more prophets, Simeon and Anna, publicly worshiped God for starting the fulfillment of the Old Testament promises—the redemption of Jerusalem, glory for the people of Israel, and redemption for all people worldwide—all of which had been foreshadowed or prophesied in the Old Testament.

These connections about who Jesus is and how he fulfills the Old Testament promises are made even more explicit in John 1:1–18. The opening phrase of this chapter, "In the beginning," deliberately echoes the same first words in Genesis 1. There, those words are used to introduce God's creating actions and his immense power revealed simply by his word. Here too these words introduce God's saving actions and his immense power revealed by *the* Word, as Jesus is referred to in this passage.

Several themes, ideas, and insights can be gained through exploration of this title of Jesus as "the Word." Jesus as the Word is the ultimate communication of God to us. The Greek word that is used here *logos,* from which we get *logic* and the idea of the mind and reason. By using this word, the Greeks would have meant the rational principle that governs all things. In the Old Testament, this word is used for God's creating and sustaining power. (For example, Psalm 33:6 says, "Your Word, O Lord, is eternal; it stands firm in the heavens.") It is not only one action but a continuing action leading to the governing of the universe. Finally, in Hebrews 1:1–2, the author explains, "In the past God spoke to our forefathers through the prophets at many times and in various ways, but in these last days he has spoken to us by his Son, whom he appointed heir of all things and through whom he made the universe." The phrase "through the prophets at many times and in various ways" (verse 1) is balanced simply by "Son" (verse 2). God has communicated to us once and for all in his son, literally "in Son revelation," indicating both the person and the type. This Word *is* God and is *distinct from* God, and this Word brings light and life as he has explained or translated or narrated God. John the Baptist testified to him, but as great as John was, Jesus is superior.

The verses contained in John 1:14–18 bear clear and abundant references to the Old Testament, especially with Exodus 32–34. One of the most startling of these is the fact that in verse 14, John says that "the Word became flesh and made his dwelling among us." The word there is an echo of the word *tabernacle,* which in the Old Testament was the physical manifestation of the presence of God amid the people. Jesus has quite literally *tabernacled* among us, fulfilling the theme developed in the Old Testament of tabernacle or temple. God is with his people once and for all. All of the promises to the patriarchs that "I will be with you and will be your God" are fulfilled in Jesus!

Another link goes back to Exodus 34:6. There, Moses had boldly asked God to show his full glory. In response, God hid Moses in the cleft of a rock and passed in front of him, proclaiming,

"The LORD, the LORD, the compassionate and gracious God, slow to anger, abounding in love and faithfulness." "Love and faithfulness" there include specific words that mean gracious love and faithfulness to himself or being true to himself. So in verse 14, when John says that we have seen his glory, the disciples physically saw in Jesus the glory of God, something that Moses could not see except just slightly and while hidden in a safe place. And that phrase "love and faithfulness," translated slightly differently, can be rendered "grace and truth" in verse 17.

John begins and ends this opening to his gospel by affirming the deity of Jesus. He calls him God in verse 1 and "God the One and Only" in verse 18, but once again, both times he is both God and distinct from God. Jesus is the second person of the Trinity, both one with and separate from God, in a mystery that we may never truly understand but which draws us into the glory and majesty of God. In any case, John leaves absolutely no room—either here or in the rest of his gospel—for Jesus to be a good moral teacher or a prophet like we saw in the Old Testament. He is something altogether different, the supreme manifestation of God on earth, the only mediator or representative we will ever need.

This idea of Jesus being our one mediator or representative, fulfilling even more Old Testament types, can be seen in Luke 4. When Jesus was tempted by the devil in the desert for forty days, it reminds the reader of the people of Israel wandering in the desert for forty years—except this time, instead of unbelief and sin, Jesus responded with faith and trust in God. Every one of the scriptures that he quotes in response to the temptations is from the time that Israel was wandering in the desert, showing their *true* application. Additionally, this temptation could also remind the reader of the temptation of Adam, who succumbed and fell in rebellion to God. Jesus here is portrayed as the *true* Adam and the *true* Israel, fulfilling all that those were meant to be.

Later in this chapter, in vv. 16–22, this idea comes up again when Jesus reads at the temple from the passage in Isaiah 61. The words he applies to himself were from a passage that originally spoke of the coming Anointed One (see day 18). But what he says here—that he has been anointed to preach good news to the poor, proclaim freedom for the captives, and proclaim the year of the Lord's favor—is what Israel was originally designed to do. Where Israel failed in this task, Jesus would not fail. Indeed, immediately after this, we see him driving out evil spirits and healing many people.

Finally, Jesus gives two Old Testament examples, from the prophets Elijah and Elisha, about God's concern for Gentiles. Remember that one of the purposes of God calling out Israel in the Old Testament was to be a light to the Gentiles and to live out God's kingdom on earth so that others could see it and be drawn to the One True God. But where they failed and turned inward or simply assimilated with the culture around them, Jesus would go on to be the Savior of the world, both Jew and Gentile.

With Jesus portraying himself as the *true* Israel—wholly fulfilling all the purposes and missions of Israel—he also fulfilled the office of *true* King, proclaiming the kingdom of God and himself as its king. Matthew 5–7 shows us the inaugural address of this king, known to us as the Sermon on the Mount. Before we get into Jesus's teaching here, the first two verses provide some significant context for the importance of the Sermon on the Mount. "Now when he saw the crowds, he went up on a mountainside and sat down. His disciples came to him, and he began to teach them" (Matthew 5:1–2). There were crowds following him because of his miraculous signs and wonders, but the primary audience here was his disciples, those whom he had called. When Jesus sits down, Matthew may be portraying him as a King sitting on his throne (see Psalm 80:1–2, Psalm 99:1, Hebrews 1:3). To refer again to the verse we read earlier in Hebrews, "after he had provided purification for sins, he sat down at the right hand of the throne of the majesty in heaven" (1:3). It was also common for Jewish rabbis to sit down when they were teaching, linking him to cultural and religious traditions of his day.

Finally, the setting of the mountainside also links to other parts of the Bible. Later, Jesus's transfiguration and Great Commission to his disciples will occur on mountainsides. Most importantly, however, this is both a parallel and a contrast to when God spoke to Moses, giving him the Ten Commandments on Mount Sinai. Both were addresses to people the Lord had called. Both laid out expectations for members of that kingdom. And both are more indicative of those who are redeemed, rather than a way to reach moral perfection or get to God. But whereas in the Old Testament the law was given only to one person, in terrifying smoke and thunder, here this message is addressed to many people, through the one who brought grace and truth, as we read in John 1.

Then Jesus begins to teach this "new" law. The idea of a separation in the Old Testament between moral law, ceremonial law, and civil law is common, particularly in trying to understand the complicated nature of the relationship between the law and the Gospel. But here, Jesus makes no such distinction. In verse 18, he simply says that he has not come to abolish the law but to fulfill it. But what did this mean? Did he deepen the law? Keep it? Nullify it? It is important to remember that the idea of "righteousness by faith" was in place *before* the law was given at Mount Sinai. All the way back in Genesis 15, Abraham believed God, and it was credited to him as righteousness. God did not choose the nation of Israel based on their observance of the law. Rather, he gave them the law as the covenant regulations for how a sinful people could dwell with a holy God. And Jesus fulfilled every part of the law by living in complete obedience to the Father. He lived the life we should have lived, and he would eventually die the death that we deserved to die.

So why did God give the law at all? First, the law served as a kind of schoolmaster, as Paul states in Galatians 3:24. It established paradigms for the temple, tabernacle, and priesthood, acting as a tutor that prepared the Jewish mind for Christ. The law was never intended to save; the Old Testament narrative itself shows us that anything besides dependence on and trust in God is futile. Many of the prophets condemn the people for outwardly fulfilling the requirements of the law while ignoring its heart for justice, peace, and serving the one true God. At its most basic level, the moral requirements of the law provide the groundwork for how life in the kingdom of God was to operate. But here, in the Sermon on the Mount, Jesus takes them deeper.

The content of his teaching showed the character of a disciple in the Beatitudes (blessed are those in right relationship with God and others), ethical admonitions at the heart level (such as equating murder with hate and adultery with lust), and contrasts between Jesus's teaching and Jewish legalistic practices, which often were harmful to the marginalized or oppressed. As a whole, Jesus teaches his listeners to seek first the kingdom of God, giving some specifics as to what that looks like. The whole Sermon on the Mount is, in effect, King Jesus's inaugural address, proclaiming that the kingdom of God has come in him.

Our next passage takes us to a conversation between Jesus and one who recognized this kingdom but wasn't sure how it could work. In John 3, we see Jesus encounter a highly regarded Jewish teacher named Nicodemus and explain to him that he must be born again. He was Israel's teacher, wealthy, learned, probably noble, and likely had most of the Old Testament memorized. In verses 1–2, he recognized *something* of the kingdom of God in Jesus, but Jesus's response to him was completely unexpected. At first, Nicodemus takes this rebirth literally and is understandably skeptical of the mechanics involved. Then his response turns to incredulity. "How can this be?" In essence, he is saying, "You ask or promise too much, Jesus. That is impossible." The desire to start over is endemic in all of us, but where should Nicodemus have found this idea? Jesus asks him, "You are Israel's teacher, and you do not understand these things?" (verse 10), indicating that at least the hints, if not fully fledged ideas, were all throughout the Old Testament, especially to someone who knew it as well as he would have.

Consider all that we have seen in the Old Testament, from the covenant promises to the idea of a new creation. Consider especially the Isaiah passages that spoke of the kingdom of God on earth and the complete forgiveness of sins. Consider the Jeremiah passage that spoke of a new covenant. Finally, consider Ezekiel 36:25–27 (which echoes that Jeremiah passage) where the Lord says to Israel, "I will sprinkle clean water on you, and you will be clean; I will cleanse you from all of your impurities and from all of your idols. I will give you a new heart and put a new spirit in you; I will remove from you your heart of stone and give you a heart of flesh. And I will put my Spirit in you and move you to follow my decrees and be careful to keep my laws." Again, Nicodemus's deep familiarity with the entire Old Testament should have pointed him at least to these ideas, but Jesus as the Messiah still would have been unexpected in all of the ways he fulfilled the Old Covenants.

This week, we have seen an astounding number of Old Testament themes and types fulfilled in the coming of Jesus. While the Old Testament paved the way for him and ideally prepared the hearts and minds of the people, they were more looking for a Messiah who would come in power and free Israel from political oppression. But instead, the God of the universe came as a baby. Through his life and ministry so far, we have seen Jesus as the embodiment of many Old Testament themes. He was the *true* people of God—everything God had intended Israel to be. He was the *true* prophet—not only preaching the word but being the Word. He was the *true* king—descended from David and the representative of the kingdom of God.

In all of these roles, he served as one representing the many. Next week, we will see this same idea but in different forms: Jesus as our true priest, as our true sacrifice, and as our true substitutionary atonement. Next week, one life will be given in ransom for many. And next week, we will see Jesus as our *true* Covenant Lord.

Days 26–30

Key Themes: Now that these themes have been developed in the Old Testament, take note of how they are continued or fulfilled in the New Testament.

Creation	Redemption	David	Shepherd
Kingdom	Passover Lamb	Jerusalem	Restoration
Representative	Holiness (law)	Temple	Israel
Substitute	Priest		Messiah
"First Gospel"	Sacrifice		Suffering Servant
Covenant	King		Glorious King
Yahweh/Lord	Prophet		

26

JOHN 5, 11

In **John 5**, Jesus makes several audacious claims about himself after performing a particularly audacious deed. This chapter alone dispels any notion that Jesus thought of himself simply as a good teacher. First, he cured a man who had been an invalid for thirty-eight years simply by the word of his power. Then he explained his actions to the Jewish leaders in such a way that they "tried all the harder to kill him" (v. 18). Several specific instances are worth noting.

First, in verses 20–23, Jesus places himself (the Son) on equal ground as God (the Father) in the areas of giving life, raising the dead, judging others, and receiving honor. These acts were normally only accorded to God the Father and would have been utter blasphemy from the mouth of anyone but one who was equal to God in every way. Furthermore, Jesus ascribes to himself the power to grant eternal life to those who hear his word and believe in him. He has "life in himself" (v. 26) and is not dependent on anyone else. Rather, through his universal authority, he can bring life to others.

Jesus goes on to claim in verses 36–37 that not only did John the Baptist testify about him, but God himself has testified about him as well. If anyone claims to believe in God the Father but not Jesus the Son, they have to ignore this part of God's testimony. And in verses 39–40 and 45–47, Jesus states that the whole of the Old Testament scriptures points to him. It is not enough to simply read and understand the scriptures; we must see the "light of the gospel of the glory of Christ" (2 Corinthians 4:4) in them.

Then in **John 11,** both Jesus's full humanity and full deity (or God-ness) are on display. We see him weep with his friends at the death of Lazarus and then miraculously raise him from the dead. Verses 25–26 encapsulate his teachings on this. He says to Martha, "I am the resurrection and the life. He who believes in me will live, even though he dies, and whoever lives and believes in me will never die. Do you believe this?"

Jesus does not simply say that he *gives* resurrection and life, as amazing as that alone would be. Rather, he states it as part of his identity. "*I am* the resurrection and the life." These words also call to mind God's proclamation of his name to Moses in the burning bush as "*I am*" (see reading for day 5). His nature is such that final death is impossible for him, as it is for all those who believe in his name. We will experience a physical death, but the deeper life that Jesus gives means that death will be unable to triumph in the end.

Martha's response to Jesus is a beautiful confession of faith. "I believe that you are the Christ, the Son of God, who was to come into the world" (v. 27). Even amid her grief at the death of her brother and her confusion over why Jesus didn't come earlier, she knew that this Jesus was the promised Messiah, the one equal to God himself. She placed her trust fully in him, and he did not disappoint her.

Notes

Read: Summarize what you read today. Write down any questions you have about the passage.

Reflect: What do you learn about God in these chapters, and/or what do you learn about people? How do these chapters contribute to the overall story line of the Bible? What key themes are developed or fulfilled here? (Refer to the list at the beginning of the week for help.)

Respond: Why were the Jewish leaders so upset with the claims that Jesus was making? When has physical death seemed to triumph in your life, and how does this passage speak truth into those times? Do you agree with Martha's confession of who Jesus is? Are there aspects of Jesus's claims about himself that you find hard to accept?

27

Day

JOHN 15, 17

In the narrative of the book of John, chapters 1–12 detail his works and his words, and in chapter 13, he gathers with his disciples for the Last Supper before his crucifixion. Chapters 14–17 are all spoken to his close disciples on the eve of his death. Put in this context, these chapters, including today's reading, are directed specifically to those who know Christ and desire to follow him more deeply.

The first part of **John 15** records Jesus describing himself as the true vine, and his followers as the branches. In the Old Testament, the nation of Israel was often referred to as a vine—but a corrupt vine that bore little fruit (see, for example, Psalm 80:8–16, Isaiah 5:1–7, and Jeremiah 2:21). That vine did not fulfill its purpose, but Jesus, the true vine, did. Now true believers, the branches, must remain connected to the vine. Each branch receives its life and nourishment and very existence from being connected to the vine. The repeated injunction to *abide* or *remain* emphasizes the necessity of this for bearing fruit: good works, obedience to his commands, love for others, and a godly life.

Jesus also explains to his disciples that to love God means to obey him (verses 9–10) and that this is ultimately for our full and complete joy (verse 11). His commands can be summed up in verse 12. "Love each other as I have loved you." But he also explains that we have him to look to as our example. "Greater love has no one than this, that he lay down his life for his friends" (verse 13). Jesus provided the ultimate example for us in obeying God, loving him, and loving others through his sacrificial death on the cross. This will not be popular with the world, and they will turn on the disciples in hatred. But together with the Spirit, the Counselor (verse 26), followers of Jesus can testify about his goodness and his love and his grace, ultimately bringing glory to the Father.

After we see this teaching, we get a precious glimpse into the prayer life of Jesus in **John 17**. Just before he is betrayed and crucified, he prays for himself, for his disciples, and for all future believers.

When he prays for himself, the connected glory of Jesus and the Father is revealed. He also once again points to his mission when he says, "Now this is eternal life: that they may know you, the only true God, and Jesus Christ, whom you have sent" (v. 3). This echoes back to the reading for day 20, where John 3:16 famously declares that those who believe in Jesus will have eternal life. And now, this verse clarifies what that eternal life is: *knowing God.*

Jesus then moves on to pray for his disciples. He prays for their protection, for their joy, and for their sanctification. He does not pray that they would leave the world, even though they do not belong to it, for he is sending them into the world just as he was sent (vv. 15–18). And as they are sent, he specifically indicates how he wants them to be sanctified or made holy: by the truth of God's word (v. 17). It is impossible to remain in him or be made holy apart from his Word.

Finally, Jesus prays for all future believers, including those of us who follow Jesus today. The crux of this prayer is on the unity of believers. The oneness of those who follow him echoes the oneness of Jesus and the Father, and in turn it reflects to the world that Jesus was truly sent by God (v. 23). Since this is the last of Jesus's discourse before his arrest, the importance of this prayer for unity cannot be overstated. Jesus prayed for *our* unity. May our churches, homes, and lives be an answer to this prayer.

Notes

Read: Summarize what you read today. Write down any questions you have about the passage.

Reflect: What do you learn about God in these chapters, and/or what do you learn about people? How do these chapters contribute to the overall story line of the Bible? What key themes are developed or fulfilled here? (Refer to the list at the beginning of the week for help.)

Respond: In your life, what does it practically mean to "remain" or "abide" in Jesus, and how are you doing with this? What fruit are you seeing in your life or in the lives of people in your church or small group? What do you think it means to know God, and how is this connected to eternal life? How can you contribute to the unity that Jesus prayed for?

28

Day

MATTHEW 26-27

To the eyes of those who saw it, Jesus's life and ministry ended in shame, betrayal, mockery, pain, and rejection. This was it. The disciples had been fooled. His followers were scattered. And everyone who had placed their trust in Jesus was disappointed.

But this death was no accident. This was, in fact, the very reason why Jesus came. Go back to day 18 and reread Isaiah 53. Remember that this chapter was written hundreds of years before Jesus walked the earth. Yet it summarized the nature and purpose of his death perfectly. This suffering servant, this would-be Messiah, was "despised and rejected" (verse 3). He "took up our infirmities and carried our sorrow" (v. 4). And in all this, "he was pierced for our transgressions, he was crushed for our iniquities; the punishment that brought us peace was upon him, and by his wounds we are healed" (v. 5).

Paul would later explain that "the wages of sin is death" (Romans 6:23) and that God is both "just and the one who justifies" (Romans 3:26). The sin of each person who has ever lived was upon Jesus that day, and he acutely felt the separation that it caused him from his Father. Someone had to pay the penalty of sin. The idea of a sacrificial offering—one life offered in place of another—had been in place since God covered Adam and Eve with animal skins after the fall (see day 2). But here, it is *God himself* who is paying the price. How many times in our Old Testament readings did we see God affirm again and again that the penalty of breaking the covenant would be on *him?* (See, for example, day 3.) As a just God, he would not stand for injustice—sin demands death—but instead of *our* eternal death, it was the death of *Jesus* that accomplished this.

The disciples and those who saw, however, did not yet understand these things. For three days, they lived in complete darkness of the soul. They did not yet realize that this *had* to happen, that this was God's plan all along, that "by his wounds, we are healed."

Notes

Read: Summarize what you read today. Write down any questions you have about the passage.

Reflect: What do you learn about God in these chapters, and/or what do you learn about people? How do these chapters contribute to the overall story line of the Bible? What key themes are developed or fulfilled here? (Refer to the list at the beginning of the week for help.)

Respond: What do you think that Peter, Joseph of Arimathea, Mary, Judas, or some of the other people in these chapters would have been thinking and feeling? Why did Jesus die, and what implications does this have for you and those around you? What aspect of Jesus's death is most meaningful to you?

29
Day

JOHN 20

Mary Magdalene walked to Jesus's tomb in sadness and in deep grief. She was prepared to care for his body, to mourn him, and to process through some of her confusion. But unexpectedly, the tomb was empty. What could this mean? Her natural response was to assume that someone moved the body. The idea of resurrection was so far from her mind that she did not immediately recognize Jesus when he stood in front of her.

But when he called her by name, she did.

With great joy and surprise, she ran to the other disciples to tell them the news. No one fully understood the significance of what had happened (see v. 9), but when Jesus later appeared to the disciples as well, they were "overjoyed" (v. 20) to see him. Peter was among these disciples—the first time seeing Jesus since denying him three times on the night of his death—and Jesus welcomed him back in (see John 21:15–25). And when Thomas demanded to see proof before he would believe, Jesus gladly showed him his scars.

Much of the remainder of the New Testament writings are spent unpacking the theological and practical significance of the resurrection. And John closes this chapter by explaining the whole purpose of these events. "These are written that you may believe that Jesus is the Christ, the Son of God, and that by believing you may have life in his name" (v. 25). This author had a definite purpose in mind, and he understood that what he had seen would change *everything*. Rest for a moment in the overwhelming, life-changing, world-altering *joy* that the disciples and their friends experienced when they realized that Jesus was alive and that "it was impossible for death to keep its hold on him" (Acts 2:24). Jesus is risen. He is risen indeed!

Notes

Read: Summarize what you read today. Write down any questions you have about the passage.

Reflect: What do you learn about God in these chapters, and/or what do you learn about people? How do these chapters contribute to the overall story line of the Bible? What key themes are developed or fulfilled here? (Refer to the list at the beginning of the week for help.)

Respond: Now, three days later, what do you think Peter, Mary, or the other people in this chapter would have been thinking and feeling? What elements of the resurrection are most surprising, confusing, or important to you? Do you believe that Jesus is the Christ, the Son of God, and by believing, do you have life in his name?

30

LUKE 24

Any event recounted by multiple people today would contain different details of what happened. Here too we see different details from Luke's account of the resurrection. But the grieving walk to the tomb, the surprising emptiness, and the life-changing appearances of Jesus himself are as evident here as they were in yesterday's reading.

Luke also includes a few additional pieces of information about what Jesus did after his resurrection, one of which is the story of the two men on the road to Emmaus first highlighted in the introduction to this study. Jesus, unrecognized by the men, walked with them for some time and pretended not to know what had been going on in Jerusalem. After the men explained the situation, Jesus responded in an unexpected way. "'How foolish you are, and how slow of heart to believe all that the prophets have spoken! Did not the Christ have to suffer these things and then enter his glory?' And beginning with Moses and all the Prophets, he explained to them what was said in all the Scriptures concerning himself" (vv. 25–27). Jesus knew that these Jewish men would have been very familiar with the Old Testament scriptures, and he expected them to recognize from those scriptures that the Messiah would suffer and be raised from the dead (see also v. 46, Psalm 22, Isaiah 53).

This passage points to a continuing truth, as we saw back in the introduction to this study: *all* of scripture points toward Jesus, to the glory of God. From beginning to end, this story of creation, rebellion, redemption, and restoration explains the need for and the work of Jesus Christ. He echoed this once more to his disciples. "Everything must be fulfilled that is written about me in the law of Moses, the Prophets, and the Psalms" (v. 44). But the text continues that "he opened their minds so they could understand the Scriptures" (v. 45). The glory of God is revealed in his Word, but he also works in our hearts to enable us to see this glory (see days 20 and 22). And then, forty days after his resurrection, with a final commission to be witnesses of these things, Jesus ascended into heaven, leaving his disciples worshiping and praising God.

Notes

Read: Summarize what you read today. Write down any questions you have about the passage.

Reflect: What do you learn about God in these chapters, and/or what do you learn about people? How do these chapters contribute to the overall story line of the Bible? What key themes are developed or fulfilled here? (Refer to the list at the beginning of the week for help.)

Respond: What new details of the resurrection stuck out to you in today's reading? In what ways have you seen all of scripture point to the person and work of Jesus? Ask God to open your heart so that you can understand the scriptures more.

Days 26–30: Summary and Teaching

Last week, we saw the fulfillment of many Old Testament themes and types with Jesus as true Israel, prophet, and king. We looked at how the birth of Jesus was surprising but also how Jesus expected those familiar with the law and the prophets to recognize who he was. And we saw that from even before his birth, he was no mere man. He was God. This week, we continued to see Jesus fulfilling themes and types from the Old Testament as true priest, sacrifice, substitutionary atonement, and covenant Lord. We read in John 5 and 11 about his teaching and his miracles, including raising Lazarus from the dead. In John 15 and 17, we saw his special teaching to the disciples and his prayer before he was arrested. In Matthew 26–27, we read the account of his suffering and his death on the cross. In John 20, we saw him resurrected, and in Luke 24, he ascended to heaven. These familiar events of Jesus's ministry, teaching, life, death, resurrection, and ascension changed everything from the Old Covenant into the New Covenant. Let's take a deeper look at the significance of these events and how they relate to the overall story line of the Bible.

The gospel according to John is unique among the four accounts of Jesus's life. Whereas Matthew, Mark, and Luke record the life of Jesus in a more narrative style, leaving some of the fuller significance of Jesus's miracles and actions underdeveloped, John focuses more on the theology behind the person and work of Jesus. A few signs and miracles are recorded, but they are immediately followed by a discourse on their importance or significance. Almost every chapter in the book of John contains some affirmation, whether direct or subtle, about Jesus's Godness, or deity.

John 5 is a perfect example of these patterns. The chapter opens with an account of Jesus healing a man who had been an invalid for thirty-eight years simply by telling him to pick up his mat and walk. The Jewish leaders, however, saw only that this healing had taken place on the Sabbath, so an extended discussion begins from that, with Jesus explaining why he has the authority to do what he did. The Jews claim that the man who had been healed was also breaking the Sabbath because he was carrying his mat. However, as we mentioned last week in Jesus's teaching in the Sermon on the Mount, the Jewish teachers and leaders often added undue burdens to the law through their interpretation. Both here and throughout the gospels, Jesus made it clear that it was *always* lawful to do good and to save life—including on the Sabbath.

The Jews, however, did not accept this, and they began to persecute him. His response in verse 17 is curious. "My Father is always at his work to this very day, and I, too, am working." Something in this response was weighty enough that verse 18 says, "For this reason, the Jews tried all the harder to kill him; not only was he breaking the Sabbath, but he was even calling God his own Father, making himself equal with God." What did Jesus say that was so offensive to them?

Today, sonship is largely biological, but in ancient times, the business of the family was carried on by the family. And much of a son's training would be received from his family. The overwhelming majority would do what their parents did. So sonship claims point to who a person is identified with—where their training, authority, and expertise come from. By claiming God as his Father—a title that would have been considered inappropriately intimate—Jesus was making an identity claim: a strong enough claim that the Jews wanted to kill him. They well understood that this was a claim to be equal to God, and they viewed it as blasphemy, which it is—unless it is true.

In the debate that follows, Jesus continues this idea, taking the issue from working on the Sabbath to who he really is. The Jews admitted that God could "work" on the Sabbath in the sense of him carrying on the "work" of upholding and maintaining the universe, so that all of creation would not fall into disarray in one day out of every seven. God can work on the Sabbath because he is God; Jesus is excused only if he himself is God, which is exactly correct. Jesus's actions are coextensive with the actions of the Father (v. 19). There is uniformity of will and purpose between the Father and Son (v. 23). And the Father has granted the Son to have life in himself and to give life wherever he pleases (v. 26)—as we also saw when Jesus raised Lazarus from the dead in John 11. Above all, the fact that Jesus has this special, unique relationship with the Father—echoing back to John 1:1, where the Word, or Jesus, was both with God and was God—gives him the right to heal and to save, even on the Sabbath.

One other thing to point out from this chapter comes from verses 39–40, where Jesus tells the Jewish leaders, "You diligently study the Scriptures because you think that by them you possess eternal life. These are the Scriptures that testify about me, yet you refuse to come to have life." Simply put, Jesus is the fulfillment of the Old Testament. If his role as Messiah isn't affirmed, neither is the entire biblical faith. Failure to confess Christ is failure to confess Yahweh.

John 11 continues this theme as well, particularly when Jesus tells Martha in verses 25–26, "I am the resurrection and the life. He who believes in me will live, even though he dies, and whoever lives and believes in me will never die." Jesus is again making *radical* claims about himself and his authority. There is no doubt whatsoever that he saw himself as the complete fulfillment of the Old Testament, and he expects those who believe in him to believe this as well.

The first twelve chapters of the book of John recount signs and miracles with their accompanying theological discourses, explaining the significance of who Jesus is and why he has come. Then the book shifts, and in John 13–17, we have a lengthy section of Jesus talking only to his disciples on the night he is to be betrayed. The discussion here is some of the most precious and intimate moments that we get of Jesus, and our reading in John 15 and 17 is no exception. John 15:1 records Jesus saying, "I am the true vine, and my Father is the gardener." This is one of seven "I am" statements found throughout the book of John. The phrase "I am" echoes back to Exodus 3, where God revealed himself to Moses as "I AM WHO I AM." Once again, we see this continuation of the Mosaic covenant here in Jesus; once again, to accept Jesus's claims about himself is to trust Yahweh, the covenant God of Abraham, Isaac, and Jacob.

Additionally, the "vine" metaphor was used multiple times in the OT to describe Israel (see Psalm 80:8–16, Isaiah 5:1–7, Jeremiah 2:21), but that vine is always lacking in some way, usually not bearing fruit as it was designed to do. Jesus, however, is the *true* Israel as we saw last week. He is the *true* vine, living the life we should have lived. Jesus instructs his followers to remain, or abide, in him, bearing fruit as the branches of that true vine. Two examples of what this looks like, according to verses 9–17, are to love God and each other and to keep his commandments—the same heart behind the Old Testament law, though many aspects looked different with Jesus. Jesus also explains in this discourse that the Counselor, the Holy Spirit, was going to come and guide the disciples after he had gone. This event will not occur until after Jesus's death, resurrection, and ascension, but he speaks of it here to let his disciples know what will happen.

Jesus continues these themes, instructions, and encouragements to his disciples through chapter 16, and then in chapter 17, his focus turns heavenward. Here we have a glimpse into what the prayers of Jesus looked like. Jesus prays for himself, for his disciples, and for all of the believers who would come later. For himself, he prays that he would be glorified that he might ultimately bring glory to his Father. He also says that the work he has been sent to do is almost complete. For his disciples, those who believe his teaching and who he is, he prays for protection, for joy, and for sanctification by the truth of his word. He doesn't pray for them to be taken out of the world but that they would be protected from the evil one. For all believers—including us today—Jesus prays for unity, for love, and for deeper knowledge of him.

These teachings, this prayer, were the last words of Jesus that John recorded before his arrest. Jesus knew what was going to happen to him, and he knew why he was doing it. He was going to his death so that his disciples—both then and now—could have eternal life. And as he said in John 17:3, "Now this is eternal life: that they may know you, the only true God, and Jesus Christ, whom you have sent." Everything that was about to occur was so that we might know God and know his one and only Son. Everything was so that we might have *life* in his name.

But first, the author of life had to become subject to death. In these crucial chapters of the story line of the Bible, we see Jesus as the true priest and true sinless sacrifice. He willingly gave his life as a ransom for many and in doing so provided the justification for our sins and secured our way to God (see Mark 10:45, Luke 22:19–20, John 10:11, 15). So how was this done?

This had been the plan all along. In Matthew 26:24, Jesus says that "the Son of Man will go just as it is written about him." He probably was talking about Isaiah 53, which predicted the suffering servant who would bear the sin of many. God was in control the whole time. This was no accident; this was the plan from all the way back in Genesis 3:15. There, when cursing the serpent, God had said that there would be enmity between him and the offspring of the woman, that he would strike his heel, but that the offspring of the woman would crush his head. Here in these chapters, we essentially see the serpent striking his heel, delivering a wound that would harm but not ultimately destroy.

Again, in verses 53–54, Jesus explicitly states that he could have called tens of thousands of angels to rescue him from the current circumstances, but that he had to do this so that the scriptures would be fulfilled. How trivial his arrest must have seemed to him! But he chose to go through with his humiliating and excruciating arrest, betrayal, suffering, and death—for you and for me. He lived the life we should have lived and died the death we deserved to die. God, in his justice, could not leave the sins of humans undealt with. In that case, evil and injustice would win. Instead, in an ultimate, unthinkable combination of justice and mercy, his wrath was poured out on his one and only Son instead of on us.

Jesus was the true sinless offering, issuing in the new covenant, and he knew this. On the night he was betrayed, he took the bread and broke it, saying, "Take and eat; this is my body" (v. 26). And he took the cup and said, "Drink from it, all of you. This is my blood of the covenant, which is poured out for many for the forgiveness of sins" (vv. 27–28). This statement clarified the purpose and significance of what was about to occur. Ever since Adam and Eve rebelled against God in the garden, the shedding of blood was required, since, as Leviticus 17:17 put it, "the life of the creature is in its blood." The shedding of blood represented a life for a life, or the idea of substitutionary atonement. When Adam and Eve sinned, an animal had to be killed so that they could be covered. When God asked Abraham to offer up Isaac, he provided a ram to be killed instead. When the angel of death passed over the people of Israel during the tenth plague, it was because the blood of a lamb had been spread on the doorways of their homes.

These examples of substitutionary atonement were sufficient for the time being but had to be repeated again and again. The blood of bulls and goats could cleanse a person externally for a short time. But here, we have the Son of God himself, the true and perfect sacrifice, our spotless substitute, the true Passover Lamb, taking our place once and for all. This bloodshed not only linked back to previous covenants; it fulfilled them completely. He even took the full curse of the law upon himself, since Deuteronomy 11:26–28 indicates that anyone hung on a cross was cursed. He took the full weight of sin, the full curse of the law, and the full obligations of the Old Testament covenant. And with the perfect sacrifice of himself, this royal Son of David, Son of Man, and Son of God finished the work once and for all.

God made this even more clear with the tearing of the curtain in the temple. Matthew 27:51 indicates that at the moment of Jesus's death, "the curtain of the temple was torn in two from top to bottom." Under the Old Covenant, this curtain had separated the Holy Place from the Most Holy Place. Several weeks ago, we talked about the requirements for the high priest on the Day of Atonement (see day 8), where once per year he—and he alone—could enter the presence of God after detailed cleansing rituals and after offering sacrifices for his own sins, so that he could then represent the people. But here, on this *ultimate* Day of Atonement, our great high priest entered the Most Holy Place on our behalf and by his death tore open the curtain, giving us direct access to God the Father for all of eternity. Long ago, God had promised Abraham that he would be his God and would dwell with him. Here in Jesus, we have God in the flesh, and by his death, he gave us access to the Father so that he can truly be our God and we his people. This darkest of days truly was a Good Friday.

The disciples clearly did not grasp any of this on the day of Jesus's death. All they knew was that this one they had followed, this one that they had put their hope in, was dead. Little did they know that what they would experience that Sunday would change the course of history and forever alter the way that people related to God. John 20 records Mary Magdalene discovering the tomb empty when she went to honor his body. When she saw that he wasn't there, her first thought was not resurrection. It was thievery. Verse 9 also indicates that Peter and John "still did not understand from Scripture that Jesus had to rise from the dead." As surely as his death had been in the hands of God from the beginning, so was his resurrection.

When the disciples finally saw Jesus, they were overjoyed and believed in him. Thomas, however, wasn't with them at the time. When he heard about such things, he didn't believe it and said he wouldn't believe it until he saw for himself. Unfortunately, this has earned him the derisive title of "doubting Thomas." But the other disciples only believed because they had already seen Jesus. And indeed, when Jesus appeared to them again, the first thing he said to Thomas was "Put your finger here; see my hands. Reach out your hand and put it into my side. Stop doubting and believe" (20:28). This prompts Thomas's belief of not only the resurrection but also the deity of Jesus. "My Lord and my God!"

What cannot be overstated here is the importance of Jesus's bodily resurrection. Back in John 1:14, as we saw last week, John described the incarnation as the Word becoming flesh and making his dwelling among us. Those who lived at that time could see him, touch him, walk with him, and listen to him. This was the Old Testament promise of "Immanuel"—God with us—come true. Indeed, all throughout the gospel of John and the later letters of John, a major theme is "Look! See! The Messiah has come! Behold for yourselves!" Jesus invaded history. He lived in a specific historical time, geographical place, and political context. This story of redemption is not otherworldly; it is very much *thisworldly.* This is also a foretaste of what is to come in the final chapter of restoration. It is not just our souls that will be whisked away to an out-of-body paradise. When God created the world and all that is in it, he declared it good, and that same creation will somehow be restored. This includes our bodies, as exemplified in Jesus's bodily resurrection.

Not all who saw believed, and as we know today, not all who believe saw. But we have the hope of the historical, public event of the resurrection grounding our faith. Next week, we will see Paul expound even further on the importance of the bodily resurrection of Christ as the absolute cornerstone of our faith. The resurrection is the absolute linchpin of the biblical story line. Without it, Jesus's claims are meaningless and even his death had no value; we would still be in our sins. And when Thomas proclaimed, "My Lord and my God!" he recognized what we can too. Yahweh, the covenant God of Abraham, Isaac, and Jacob, the Word made flesh, the author of life, defeated death by death so that we could live in him.

More than that, 2 Corinthians 5:21 says, "God made him who had no sin to be sin for us, so that in him we might become the righteousness of God." Jesus *became* sin on our behalf, so that we might have his righteousness and therefore experience a restored relationship with God. He trampled over sin and death, fulfilled every aspect of the Old Covenants and the Old Testament in general, and rose to new life as a preview of the restoration that is yet to come!

Luke 24 gives another account of the resurrection. As with any instance of different people telling the same story, different details are emphasized, but the main ideas of the account remain the same. The same Jesus who had died and been buried was raised to life, appearing to women and to the disciples in order to show his complete victory. Luke also adds a new account, that of the two men on the road to a town called Emmaus. As they walked along, Jesus joined them, but they did not realize that it was him. He pretended not to know what was going on, so they explained who Jesus had been—"a prophet, powerful in word and deed before God and all the people" (v. 19)—but sentenced to death and killed three days earlier. Then some of the women found the tomb empty, and they simply did not know what to make of the entire situation.

Jesus responded with a sermon that could sum up this entire Bible study. He said to them, "'How foolish you are, and how slow of heart to believe all that the prophets have spoken! Did not the Christ have to suffer these things and then enter his glory?' And beginning with Moses and all the Prophets, he explained to them what was said in all the Scriptures concerning himself" (verses 25–27). His phrase "Moses and all the Prophets" was a colloquial way of saying "the entirety of the Old Testament."

Later, when he appears to his disciples, he does the same thing. He says to them, "'This is what I told you while I was still with you: Everything must be fulfilled that is written about me in the Law of Moses, the Prophets, and the Psalms.' Then he opened their minds so that they could understand the scriptures. He told them, 'This is what is written: The Christ will suffer and rise from the dead on the third day, and repentance and forgiveness of sins will be preached in his name to all nations, beginning at Jerusalem. You are witnesses of these things. I am going to send you what my Father has promised'" (vv. 44–49). Once again, we see that the disciples should have understood the nature of the gospel from the Old Testament. No one could have completely predicted all of the ways that he fulfilled it, but the signs were there from the very beginning. The grand story line of the Bible is no accident. And now, like the disciples, we too are witnesses of all that Jesus is.

The story of redemption is the story of progress toward restoration of the kingdom of God. This story came to its climax in Jesus Christ of Nazareth, Son of God and rightful king of the world. He lived the perfect life we were originally designed to live, died the death we deserved to die because of our sin, and rose again three days later. He ascended into heaven and left his new church with the promised Holy Spirit.

From the beginning, these elements have been in play. When Adam and Eve rebelled in the garden, God promised victory over the powers of evil through an offspring of the woman. When God chose Abraham, he promised that he would make him into a great nation and that his offspring would be a blessing to the whole world. When Moses led the people out of Egypt, he set forth the provision of a spotless lamb to die in place of the firstborn of the families of Israel. When God gave instructions about the law, priests, and sacrifices, he set one man to represent the many and provide purification for sins. When the people were preparing to enter the land God had promised, he spoke clearly of the offices of prophet and king and how they would specifically represent the people. When Joshua led the nation into the Promised Land, he too served as a mediator, bringing the people into a good land with blessing and order. When the Lord made his covenant with King David, he swore that a descendant of his would reign forever. When the psalmists spoke of the Anointed One, they said that his kingdom would never end and that he would rule over the nations in justice and righteousness. When the kingdom divided and the people were on the verge of exile due to their sin, Isaiah prophesied that the Anointed One would suffer on behalf of many in order to heal them. When Jeremiah spoke of a new covenant, he said that God would be with the people in an unprecedented way and that he would internalize the laws of God in the hearts of the people.

With the birth of Jesus, this new covenant was inaugurated; with his death and resurrection, it was sealed by his blood. Every word of the scriptures points to him and the completed work he has finished on the cross. Every story line, every theme, every symbol, and every type converge in Jesus!

Next week, we will see how the church grew after Jesus left and how the kingdom of God continues to push forward into the world in this restoration that is already, but not yet, complete. Once again fulfilling his promises, God will send his Holy Spirit, and through his disciples and other believers, he will build his church, bringing people into the way of life in this new covenant. Thanks be to God for his indescribable gift!

Days 31–35

Key Themes: This week we will see the implications of the fulfillment of these themes. As the church grows and the message of the gospel spreads throughout the world, note the ways that these themes are continually highlighted.

Creation	Redemption	David	Shepherd
Kingdom	Passover Lamb	Jerusalem	Restoration
Representative	Holiness (law)	Temple	Israel
Substitute	Priest		Messiah
"First Gospel"	Sacrifice		Suffering Servant
Covenant	King		Glorious King
Yahweh/Lord	Prophet		

31

· Day ·

ACTS 2

On the fiftieth day after the Sabbath of Passover week—also called Pentecost, or the Feast of Weeks (see Leviticus 23:15–16)—all of the believers were together in Jerusalem. Jesus had instructed them to stay there until they received the gift of the Holy Spirit (see Acts 1:4–5), at which point they were to be "witnesses in Jerusalem, and in all Judea and Samaria, and to the ends of the earth" (Acts 1:8). So when the Holy Spirit came upon them in the form of tongues of fire, the first thing they were able to do was to speak in other languages so that the message of Jesus could go to other nations.

When this happened, the people who witnessed it were "amazed and perplexed" (v. 12), and some accused the disciples of being drunk (v. 13). But Peter addressed the crowd and explained from the scriptures all that was going on. He used several passages from the Old Testament to discuss the promised coming of the Holy Spirit as well as the death and resurrection of Jesus, and he concluded powerfully, "Therefore let all Israel be assured of this: God has made this Jesus, whom you crucified, both Lord and Christ" (v. 36). He called his listeners to repentance and baptism for the forgiveness of their sins, and that day three thousand people became Christians (v. 41).

This was a remarkable and amazing day for the early church. But it was an equally remarkable and amazing day in the life of Peter. Not too long ago, Peter had looked into the face of Jesus after vehemently denying that he even knew him, and he went away and "wept bitterly" (Luke 22:62). Peter had always been a bit impetuous: jumping out of a boat *twice* (Matthew 14:24–33; John 21:7–8), claiming to understand a glorious transfiguration (Matthew 17:1–5), and attacking those who came to arrest Jesus (John 18:10–11). But when he was the first of the disciples to confess Jesus as the Christ, the Son of the Living God, Jesus said that he would build his church on Peter, whose name meant "rock" (Matthew 16:15–19). And even though Peter denied him, Jesus kept this promise. The resurrection of Jesus transformed Peter from a rash denier into a bold proclaimer of the gospel. He was still audacious and outspoken, but God now used these exact qualities in incredibly powerful ways in the life of the early church. Peter had seen the full glory of the resurrected Jesus, and it changed him deeply and irrevocably.

Notes

Read: Summarize what you read today. Write down any questions you have about the passage.

Reflect: What do you learn about God in these chapters, and/or what do you learn about people? How do these chapters contribute to the overall story line of the Bible? What key themes are developed or fulfilled here? (Refer to the list at the beginning of the week for help.)

Respond: How did Pentecost start a new era in the life of the church? How and why was Peter's life transformed? Have you seen your life or the lives of others changed in this way? How could you, like Peter, point someone to Jesus using the Old Testament?

32

Day

ACTS 9

After Pentecost, the early church began to grow at an incredibly rapid pace. The resurrection of Jesus had turned a localized band of followers into a worldwide movement. Through sermons, miracles, and everyday church life, the apostles and other believers spread the gospel of Jesus and began to fulfill the Great Commission (see Matthew 28:18–20). Along the way, they faced persecution from the Jewish leaders who did not believe that Jesus was the Messiah. Acts 7 records the story of the first martyr of this young church, a man named Stephen, whose death was overseen by a man named Saul. Shortly after this event, many in the church were scattered throughout Judea and Samaria due to intensified persecution in Jerusalem (Acts 8:1). However, even this was part of God's plan to reach the world, since Jesus had previously told his disciples that they would be witnesses in those exact areas (Acts 1:8).

Those who hated this new church of God continued to pursue Christians. In today's reading, Saul, the one who had given authority to the first martyrdom, set out to take prisoner anyone who said they followed Jesus. As he was on his way to Damascus, Jesus himself appeared to him and said, "Saul, Saul, why do you persecute me?" (v. 4). The church was so aligned with Jesus that to persecute *believers* was to persecute *him*. After a few days with the disciples in Damascus, this same Saul "began to preach in the synagogues that Jesus is the Son of God" (v. 20). Saul's life was so immediately transformed by his encounter with Jesus that he began to teach the truth of that which he had just been out to destroy. In time, he would travel around the Middle East and Europe planting churches, going by his Greek name of Paul. Later, he would write letters to those churches that would then become much of our New Testament.

At this moment though, others around Saul were understandably confused and concerned. This man was infamous for his persecution of Christians. Could this be a trap? Would more people get hurt or killed as a result of this man's infiltration? But God assured them regarding Saul, "This man is my chosen instrument to carry my name before the Gentiles and their kings and before the people of Israel" (v. 15). Later, Saul would write, "Christ Jesus came into the world to save sinners—of whom I am the worst. But for that very reason I was shown mercy so that in me, the worst of sinners, Christ Jesus might display his unlimited patience as an example for those who would believe on him and receive eternal life" (1 Timothy 1:15–16). God could take a man known for persecuting and killing Christians and turn him into a key pillar of his church just by one encounter with Jesus. There are no limits on the people that God can use or the lives that he can transform.

Notes
Read: Summarize what you read today. Write down any questions you have about the passage.

Reflect: What do you learn about God in these chapters, and/or what do you learn about people? How do these chapters contribute to the overall story line of the Bible? What key themes are developed or fulfilled here? (Refer to the list at the beginning of the week for help.)

Respond: How did the persecution of the church actually end up fulfilling what Jesus had spoken, and what might this indicate about hardships or persecution in our lives? Do you consider yourself, or someone you know, too far gone to be saved or used by God? How does the story of Saul's conversion speak into that?

33

Day

ACTS 17

The first part of today's reading mirrors much of the book of Acts. Paul and his companions traveled from city to city, meeting people, speaking in the synagogues, and starting or strengthening the churches. For example, in Thessalonica, the capital city of Macedonia in southeastern Europe, Paul "went into the synagogue, and on three Sabbath days he reasoned with them from the scriptures, explaining and proving that the Christ had to suffer and rise from the dead" (vv. 2–3). This sermon series must have been similar to what Jesus spoke to the men on the road to Emmaus, once again using the whole of scripture to point to Jesus as the Christ (see day 30).

Whether because of persecution or expediency, Paul and his companions never stayed in one city for too long, and the gospel continued to spread throughout Asia and Europe. In Athens, the famous cultural hub of art, philosophy, and literature, Paul took a slightly different evangelistic approach. The Athenians and other leading thinkers, members of the Areopagus, loved to listen to new ideas. So Paul started with what was already familiar to them and commented on their religious nature (vv. 22). He then used their own idol, marked "TO AN UNKNOWN GOD" (v. 23), to introduce to them the God who made this world and everything in it.

Paul explained to them that this God, whom they did not yet know, was sovereign over the details of history. "He determined the times set for them and the exact places where they should live. God did this so that men would seek him and perhaps reach out for him and find him, though he is not far from each one of us" (vv. 26–27). He even quoted the Athenians' own poets in order to make a connection to them, using what he knew of their culture as a starting point to talk about the true God and how he was set apart from their idols. This particular meeting ended when Paul briefly mentioned the resurrection. The people were divided, but some wanted further discussion and some came to believe in Jesus. As a whole, Paul's speech to the Areopagus pointed to the one true God and gave us an example for how we might speak to those around us about the Jesus we know and love.

Notes

Read: Summarize what you read today. Write down any questions you have about the passage.

Reflect: What do you learn about God in these chapters, and/or what do you learn about people? How do these chapters contribute to the overall story line of the Bible? What key themes are developed or fulfilled here? (Refer to the list at the beginning of the week for help.)

Respond: What recurring patterns do you see when Paul and his companions enter a new city? What does it mean to you that God determined the exact time and place where you should live, in order that you might know him? How can we use what we know of our culture in order to bridge the gap between those around us and the one true God?

34

Day

ACTS 26

In this chapter, we see another of Paul's evangelistic approaches: his personal testimony. Throughout his missionary journeys, Paul was often persecuted or imprisoned. (See, for example, his list of hardships in 2 Corinthians 11:21–33.) But after his most recent arrest in Jerusalem, both the Jewish and Roman ruling bodies were involved in his trials. Before appearing in the presence of King Agrippa, Paul had appealed to Caesar (Acts 25:11–12). As a Roman citizen, Paul would have had the right to appear before Emperor Nero. Nero is often remembered in history for his vicious persecution of Christians, but if Paul would have won the case currently brought against him regarding his supposed crimes against the Jewish people, it would have gained official recognition for Christianity. Much more was at stake in these trials than Paul's own freedom or safety.

This Agrippa, to whom Paul is speaking in Acts 26, was King Herod Agrippa II, the great-grandson of the Herod who tried to kill the baby Jesus in Matthew 2. The various Herods were appointed by the ruling Roman emperors and the Senate, and they were involved in the death of Jesus (Luke 23), John the Baptist (Matthew 14), and some of the other apostles. Herod Agrippa II, however, showed considerable sympathy toward Paul in allowing him to speak in his own defense and share the gospel with everyone assembled there.

Paul told his story in a calm and orderly manner, speaking freely of his upbringing, conversion, and subsequent ministry. He concluded once again with the idea that he was "saying nothing beyond what the prophets and Moses said would happen—that the Christ would suffer and, as the first to rise from the dead, would proclaim light to his own people and to the Gentiles" (vv. 22–23). And when Governor Festus shouted insults in response, Paul simply replied, "What I am saying is true and reasonable" (v. 25). He even prayed for Agrippa and told him frankly that he hoped to see him become a Christian (v. 29). God had clearly been at work in the life of Paul, and he continued to work in him now, even on such a public stage. Without getting defensive or angry, Paul simply told the story of how his own life had been changed, and in doing so, he was able to explain the person and work of Jesus Christ as the fulfillment of all of scripture.

Notes

Read: Summarize what you read today. Write down any questions you have about the passage.

Reflect: What do you learn about God in these chapters, and/or what do you learn about people? How do these chapters contribute to the overall story line of the Bible? What key themes are developed or fulfilled here? (Refer to the list at the beginning of the week for help.)

Respond: How has Paul's life been changed since meeting Jesus on the road to Damascus? What is your testimony, the story of how God has worked in your life? How can you truly and reasonably tell your story so that it points your listeners toward the person and work of Jesus?

35

Day

ROMANS 3

In today's reading, Paul uses a sobering series of Old Testament quotations to show his readers that "there is no one righteous, not even one" (v. 10). In the Bible and in our world, not one person is without sin. Regardless of upbringing, church involvement, faith, or personality, no one is able to reach God due to the wrong they have done. Each one of us is guilty of wrongdoing; Paul writes that "all have sinned and fall short of the glory of God" (v. 23). This propensity toward sin goes to our very core; indeed, when people try to justify their imperfections, they might say, "I'm only human," meaning that to be human means to be imperfect.

Some might argue that we need to embrace our imperfections and simply try to be the best versions of ourselves. We might even find that when we compare ourselves to others, we aren't nearly as bad as *that* person. But the truth is this: God is perfect and ultimately holy and our sin prevents us from ever reaching him. Even the Old Testament laws point toward this; not only could the Israelites (and by extension, us) not keep the law, but the very existence of the law reminded them of how sinful they were (v. 20). No religion, philosophy, or set of good deeds would ever be enough to reach God. All of humanity was hopelessly lost.

But then we come to a great shift in verse 21. *"But now ..."* Because people could never reach God, God has made a way for them and has testified to it all throughout the law and the prophets. He has provided a righteousness "through faith in Jesus Christ to all who believe" (v. 22). *All* have sinned, and *all* may be justified through the grace and redemption that came through Jesus's life, death, and resurrection.

Paul refers to Jesus's sacrifice as a "sacrifice of atonement, through faith in his blood" (v. 25). Since the time of the Old Testament sacrifices, the blood of one creature was taken in place of another. And so here with Jesus. The sin of humanity was a debt that needed to be paid, or God was not just. He could not let all of the evils of the earth simply slide by. But instead of requiring us to pay the penalty of death (see Romans 6:23), God took the sacrifice of Jesus in our place "to demonstrate his justice at the present time, so as to be just and the one who justifies those who have faith in Jesus" (v. 26). What a beautiful and transforming gift of justice and mercy!

Notes

Read: Summarize what you read today. Write down any questions you have about the passage.

Reflect: What do you learn about God in these chapters, and/or what do you learn about people? How do these chapters contribute to the overall story line of the Bible? What key themes are developed or fulfilled here? (Refer to the list at the beginning of the week for help.)

Respond: What is your reaction to the list of quotations in vv. 10–18? Do you consider yourself to be among the people who are described here? How has God provided a solution, and how does this reflect both his grace and his justice?

Days 31–35: Summary and Teaching

In the last couple of weeks, we have read and discussed how the person and work of Jesus Christ fulfilled many aspects of the Old Covenant. He was the climax of Old Testament themes, offices, and types, showing himself to be the *true* Son of David, the *true* priest, the *true* sacrifice, the *true* prophet, the *true* king, the *true* Israel, and more. His death and resurrection canceled the power of sin once and for all for those who believe in him, and as those in the Old Testament looked forward to the saving work of the Messiah, we now look back to that work and are reconciled to God.

This week, we looked at what happened to Jesus's followers after he ascended back into heaven, where he continually serves as our great and merciful high priest. Jesus had told them that he would not leave them alone but would give them the promised Holy Spirit as they entered the brand-new era of the church. In Acts 2, we saw Peter's great sermon following the giving of that Holy Spirit in an event called Pentecost. In Acts 9, we saw a man named Saul, who was known for persecuting Christians, come to faith in Christ after a personal encounter with Jesus. In Acts 17, we read about an example of his missionary tactics as the Word of God continued to spread. In Acts 26, we heard Saul—also called Paul—testify before the authorities on account of his faith. And in Romans 3, we saw this same Paul explain to the church in Rome what it means to be justified in Christ.

In all of these passages, we see that much has changed from the time of the Old Testament thanks to Jesus, but there was also much that did not change, including the working of Yahweh throughout history to bring people back to him in the great drama of creation, rebellion, redemption, and restoration. Let's look now at how that restoration is already beginning to be in effect and what parts remain in this already-but-not-yet tension where we currently reside.

The book of Acts is a direct continuation of the gospel of Luke, written by the same person. The opening verses of Acts 1 indicate that the former letter, the gospel of Luke, was written to inform a specific person or church about all that Jesus had done on earth. Now his task was to continue the story through the life of the early church. Much of the language used to describe the church throughout the New Testament is striking in its similarity to language used to describe Israel in the Old Testament. They are both referred to using husband-wife imagery with God and in language of a vine, a flock, the elect, a holy priesthood, and a remnant. Additionally, the church is grafted into Israel's privilege of being sons and daughters of God and being the spiritual heirs of Abraham. The church does not simply replace, nor is it identical to, Israel. But both are set apart explicitly as a kingdom of priests and a holy nation tasked with being the people of God to the eyes of the world.

In Acts 2, we see the crucial event that ushered in the birth of the church as we know it. In

Jesus, the king had come, but with the arrival of the Holy Spirit, the kingdom could begin to spread throughout the world. The ministry of the Holy Spirit was the ultimate fulfillment of and transition to the New Covenant, when God truly was with his people, changing their hearts, minds, and lives from the inside out. Back in Numbers 11:29, Moses had declared, "I wish that all the Lord's people were prophets and that the Lord would put his Spirit on them!" Multiple specific prophecies in the Old Testament looked forward to an outpouring of the Spirit (for examples, see Isaiah 32:15, 44:3; Ezekiel 39:29; or Habakkuk 2:14). And here, in his sermon in Acts 2:17–21, Peter quotes a passage from the prophet Joel showing how the coming of the Holy Spirit had long been prophesied and looked for by the people of God.

One of the first supreme marks of wickedness in the Old Testament occurred just after the great flood. People built the tower of Babel in Genesis 11. They came together for the express purpose of reaching heaven on their own and for making a name for themselves, in effect telling God, "We don't need you at all." So in response, God confused their language and scattered them among the earth. Here at Pentecost, however, in a kind of literary foil, their languages were also confused, but it was for a much grander purpose. *God's* name would be known. Others who were in Jerusalem heard their own language being spoken, indicating an acceptance of them and their people. And while these disciples would eventually also be scattered among the earth, it was as missionaries taking the great name of God with them. Additionally, the fire that rested on these disciples was also a continuation of Old Testament stories, whereby God's presence would manifest in a burning bush (see day 5) or pillar of fire.

When some people with them started to make fun of these disciples—surely they must be drunk!—Peter stood up and responded with a sermon linking Jesus and the Holy Spirit to multiple parts of the Old Testament. Through his references to Joel and to David, he powerfully showed how all of these events were under God's control. He also spoke of Jesus's death in a remarkable combination of God's sovereignty and human responsibility in verses 23–24, which read, "This man [Jesus] was handed over to you by God's set purpose and foreknowledge; and you, with the help of wicked men, put him to death by nailing him to the cross. But God raised him from the dead, freeing him from the agony of death, because it was impossible for death to keep its hold on him." He went on to explain a quote from one of David's psalms, with language too far-reaching to be directly applied to David himself, indicating that the Davidic covenant from the Old Testament was *always* pointing to Jesus—and even David knew that, though he didn't know his name! So Peter confidently declared, "God has made this Jesus, whom you crucified, both Lord and Christ" (v. 36), and the Holy Spirit's coming was proof of this. The people listening were so moved by this proclamation that three thousand people became believers that day, and they too received the gift of the Holy Spirit, as do all believers who respond to Jesus in repentance and faith.

Another person whose life was radically changed by an encounter with the risen Christ was a man named Saul, whose story we read in Acts 9. Saul was first introduced in Acts 7 as the ringleader of the first recorded Christian martyrdom, that of a man named Stephen. In his defense to the high priest who was charging him with blasphemy, Stephen had essentially recounted the story of the nation of Israel, concluding that the Jewish leaders always disregarded God's chosen representatives and that Jesus Christ, having received the same treatment, was the ultimate representative, the ultimate temple, and the ultimate Righteous One. In response, the Jewish leaders became so angry that they stoned Stephen to death under the approving eye of Saul.

This same Saul, a Jewish leader himself and trained in the ways of the Pharisees, continued to travel throughout Judea seeking followers of "the Way" (see Acts 9:2) to persecute. From a Jew's perspective, it is easy to see why these people would have essentially been seen as heretics. From within their own religion had arisen a small group of people who followed a man who spoke blasphemy, an ordinary person who claimed to be God and who died a criminal's death. Now they were claiming this person was alive? And that the entirety of the Old Testament pointed to him? Some Jewish leaders, like Saul, were so zealous for the purity of their religion that they desired to kill those who were, in their minds, defiling it. They simply didn't and couldn't believe that Jesus, a man from the backwater town of Nazareth, who was publicly executed between thieves, could be the promised Messiah that they expected to come.

But when Jesus appeared to Saul on his way to Damascus, his life changed immediately. This Jesus *so identified* with the church that to persecute his followers was to persecute him. Additionally, the bright light and the voice itself immediately indicated to Saul that he was in the presence of deity. Once Saul experienced this Jesus for himself, he changed his mission and purpose to build this new Way. Many of those who already believed were understandably skeptical and many of the Jews sought to kill him for such an abrupt change of heart. But a few men, namely Ananias and Barnabas, acted in faith that their God had changed this man, and they welcomed him in. Soon, as verse 31 indicates, "the church throughout Judea, Galilee, and Samaria enjoyed a time of peace. It was strengthened; and encouraged by the Holy Spirit, it grew in numbers, living in fear of the Lord." Saul (who later went by the Greek version of his name, Paul) continued to grow in his faith and to contribute to the church's growth as well. His letters to various churches comprise much of the rest of the New Testament, and the remainder of the book of Acts tells the stories of his life and missionary journeys.

One such missionary journey took Paul and his companions to Thessalonica, Berea, and Athens, as recorded in Acts 17. The first few verses of the chapter indicate a common strategy among these missionaries. As they traveled, they would stop in places with a well-established Jewish synagogue, beginning their preaching there. "As his custom was, Paul went into the synagogue, and on three Sabbath days he reasoned with them from the Scriptures, explaining and proving that Christ had to suffer and rise from the dead. 'This Jesus I am proclaiming to you is the Christ,' he said" (Acts 17:2–3). Just like Jesus had done both in his time on earth and with his disciples after his resurrection, Paul took the Old Testament as the starting point for understanding Jesus as the true Messiah.

Paul consistently preached this way to the Jews in these cities, explaining how God had been at work in human history from the beginning. Many believed as a result and began to follow Jesus for themselves. But just as many did not accept Jesus, many did not accept Paul's message, and he faced danger and persecution at every turn. Here in Thessalonica, for example, the author described the Jews as "jealous" (v. 5), and they accused Paul of "defying Caesar's decrees, saying that there is another king, one called Jesus" (v. 7). In this town, unlike others, they managed to avoid prison, but they slipped out of the city during the night to another town called Berea, where much of the same happened again.

After Berea, Paul went on to Athens. Five centuries earlier, this Greek city had been at the center of the world's leading discussions and progress on philosophy, education, art, and literature. Many influential minds still resided there, and according to verse 21, "all the Athenians and the foreigners who lived there spent their time doing nothing but talking about and listening to the latest ideas." For these people, this message of Jesus that Paul was proclaiming was another one of these "latest ideas," and Paul wasted no time on this opportunity. His approach with them, however, was decidedly different from in the synagogues. Instead of starting with the Old Testament and the Jewish understanding of God, he started with the religion of the city and their understanding of the gods. He linked "the God who made the world and everything in it" (v. 24) to their "unknown God," explaining his sovereignty over the lives and times of humans and his desire for a relationship with us at any cost. When he came to the resurrection of Jesus from the dead, the similarities stopped. Some scoffed at him, but others wanted to hear more.

In either case, whether he was preaching to Jews or Gentiles, Paul understood where to start in order to talk to someone about Jesus. He knew the people, he understood the culture, and he used his knowledge and observations in order to proclaim the good news about the kingdom of God. In this way, the church continued to grow as God moved in the hearts and minds of peoples from all nations—as he had promised he would throughout the Old Testament.

After three lengthy, transcontinental missionary journeys, Paul was arrested in Jerusalem and transferred to Caesarea to await trial before the governor. He first spoke to an official named Felix, then to his successor, Festus, and finally to King Herod Agrippa II in Acts 26. With each of these trials, Paul used the opportunity to preach the gospel clearly and to seek legal recognition of Christianity.

Paul began his defense by respectfully acknowledging Agrippa's authority and explaining why he was there. He said that the Jews knew how he was raised—as a devoutly religious Jew himself, and as a Pharisee, or a member of a particularly zealous and legalistic sect of Judaism. Then in verse 6, Paul claimed that it was exactly *because* of this hope in what God had promised their fathers through the law and the prophets that he was on trial today. "The promise our twelve tribes are hoping to see fulfilled as they earnestly serve God day and night" (v. 7). Here and throughout his writings in the NT, Paul is incredibly desirous of salvation for the Jews. He seems to continually be saying, "Look! Look at the Old Testament! Everything is there. You are rejecting Jesus, but all these things were written down ahead of time, and you know them. Believe in him—repent and be saved!" Later, as Paul continued his story, he told of how the encounter with Jesus on the road to Damascus led him more toward the Gentiles, but Paul's heart for his own people never diminished. It seems incorrect to say that when Paul met Jesus, he was converted to Christianity. Rather, he was transformed in his thinking; Jesus was the fulfillment of all that had come before in the Jewish law and the prophets. He was the promised Messiah from long ago and the hope of all people—both Jew and Gentile.

In this way, further on in his speech, he claimed, "I am saying nothing beyond what the prophets and Moses said would happen—that the Christ would suffer and, as the first to rise from the dead, would proclaim light to his own people and to the Gentiles" (verses 22–23). When Festus shouted at this point that Paul was out of his mind, Paul calmly replied that what he was saying was "true and reasonable" (v. 25). He even directly addressed Agrippa and asked, "Do you believe the prophets? I know you do" (v. 27). If Agrippa would have answered yes, Paul could have continued to respectfully argue for their fulfillment in Jesus; if he had answered no, he would have found himself in political hot water with devout Jews. Unable to answer, he instead asks if Paul is trying to convert him, to which Paul unapologetically answers yes.

Whether it was through reasoning with Jews in the synagogues, connecting to Gentiles in the public square, or offering his personal testimony to political leaders, Paul shared Jesus with everyone he met in a kind, respectful, and reasonable way. He pointed his listeners not only to the life, death, and resurrection of Jesus of Nazareth but also to the writings in the Old Testament that spoke of him in advance.

Another way that Paul continued to spread the message of Jesus was through his letters. His letter to the church in Rome, known to us as Romans, is a particularly logical layout of the gospel, beginning with who God is and how he has revealed himself and continuing on to the rebellion of humanity. Romans 3 in particular confronts the sin of both Jews and Gentiles alike, and it concludes with a message of justification for both Jews and Gentiles. The church in Rome was majority Gentile because the Jews had been expelled from Rome under Emperor Claudius, and when the Jews were later allowed to return, they found that they were no longer welcome in a church that had started as a Messianic Jewish sect. Paul wrote to them to explain God's plan of salvation for *all* people and to encourage unity and love, particularly since that church had not received direct teaching from an apostle.

The first part of Romans 3 uses *nine* Old Testament quotes in order to show that "Jews and Gentiles alike are all under sin" (v. 9), concluding with the damning statement that "no one will be declared righteous in [God's] sight by observing the law; rather, through the law we become conscious of sin" (v. 20). Even in the Old Testament, the law was never intended as a *means* of salvation. Remember that the law of Moses was given to the people *after* they had been redeemed from Egypt. In fact, several people, including Noah (Genesis 6:9) and Abraham (Genesis 26:5), are said to have walked with God or followed the law of God before that law was even given. Even Gentiles, apart from the law of Moses, still have the "law" of God, as Romans 2:14–15 indicates. "Indeed, when Gentiles, who do not have the law, do by nature things required by the law, they are a law for themselves, even though they do not have the law, since they show that the requirements of the law are written on their hearts, their consciences also bearing witness, and their thoughts now accusing, now even defending them." But regardless of the type of law—whether natural law, universal moral laws, decrees of conscience, or the Mosaic law given at Mount Sinai—no one can keep it, and no one can earn righteousness before God even if they could.

Amid this bleak reality, we have two great words that set up the next part of Romans, a part central to the doctrine of Christianity and precious to its followers. "But now …" (verse 21). But now *another* righteousness has been made known, apart from the law, and the law and the prophets testified to this: though *all* have sinned and fall short of the glory of God, *all* can be justified freely by his grace through the redemption that came by Jesus Christ (verses 23–24).

A crucial Old Testament link is found in verse 25, where Paul explicitly states that Jesus is our great "sacrifice of atonement." The ceremonial system of the nation of Israel, with its priests and sacrifices, had set up this idea of atonement, or offering one life in place of another. But when the Day of Atonement was established in Leviticus 17 (see day 8), it was one high priest, once a year, offering sacrifices first for his own sins and then for the sins of the people. Now, however, Jesus is our great sacrifice of atonement, and "through faith in his blood," we are counted righteous before God!

Moreover, verse 26 explains a key reason why Jesus had to die. It was God demonstrating his justice, "so as to be just and the one who justifies those who have faith in Jesus." This is a truly amazing combination. If God had simply ignored sin, he wouldn't be just. As Romans 6:23 says a few chapters later, "The wages of sin is death." Humanity is fallen, broken, and sinful, and as not one person is righteous, the just penalty is death. No one would respect—let alone love—a God who allowed injustice to reign on the earth, turning a blind eye to hurt and crime and sin. The penalty had to be paid. But to be *both* just *and* the one who justifies? This is truly amazing news. God's wrath was appeased. Some translations might use the word "propitiation," a perfect term indicating that not only is God's wrath satisfied and he is just but also that he is now for us eternally and he is justified. God counted the death of Jesus as a sacrifice of atonement, allowing us to go free as not guilty—and more than that, to be declared righteous and accepted in the sight of God through faith in his blood. This is our great justification—our great legal declaration that through Christ, God does not count our sins against us but declares us righteous. Whereas the people had been punished symbolically through the animal sacrifices of the Old Testament, Jesus now took the full punishment and imputed to us his own right standing before God (see also 2 Corinthians 5:21).

This week, we saw the kingdom of God begin to encroach upon the world. The kingdom arrived with Jesus, but it has yet to fully take over the world as it will one day. In the meantime, we live in this already-but-not-yet tension described in the New Testament. After the life, death, resurrection, and ascension of Jesus, the Holy Spirit came upon the apostles and empowered them to spread the good news throughout the known world. One man, Paul, was especially instrumental in the spread of this gospel. Through his ministry to Jews and Greeks alike, he spoke the Word of God clearly and reasonably, and through his letters to the churches, he explained the theological significance of who Jesus was and what he had done.

Throughout the readings this week, we saw multiple instances of people referring back to the law and the prophets (otherwise known as the Old Testament in general), appealing to and explaining how God had been at work since the beginning. Though the new covenant was new in scope, in glory, and in permanence, it was in many ways a fulfillment of themes, types, and promises established in the old covenants. We continue to see how the One who is sovereign over the kingdoms of men prepared the hearts and minds of his people through his unified Word.

Next week, we will wrap up this forty-day overview study. We will see how, after justification in Jesus's name, we are called to live a sanctified life set apart for God and for the work of his kingdom. We will examine some practicalities in what this looks like and see how the churches of God continued to grow and expand. Finally, we will see hints of glorification, of restoration, and of the very last chapter of the story that has already begun yet awaits its final consummation. Through every word of scripture and moment of our lives, God has remained faithful, and he will continue to remain faithful through the very last chapter.

Days 36–40

Key Themes: This week we will continue to see the fulfillment of these themes. As the story line of the Bible reaches its conclusion, note the ways that these themes are continually highlighted.

Creation	Redemption	David	Shepherd
Kingdom	Passover Lamb	Jerusalem	Restoration
Representative	Holiness (law)	Temple	Israel
Substitute	Priest		Messiah
"First Gospel"	Sacrifice		Suffering Servant
Covenant	King		Glorious King
Yahweh/Lord	Prophet		

36

Day

ROMANS 7–8

Paul's logical and linear argument in Romans continues in these two chapters. Together, they describe the realities of life in the flesh and life in the Spirit. The Christian gospel is unique in that it embodies an "already, but not yet" philosophy as seen here. Those who have trusted in the person and work of Jesus have been declared righteous in the sight of God and have conquered sin; they are legally justified and fully belong to him. At the same time, they are growing gradually over time in the image of God and battling through their sin.

Romans 7 recounts this battle in a manner familiar to anyone who seeks to walk with God. The desire to do good and to please God is counteracted by the simultaneous desire to sin and to please the self. While elements of this struggle might be present throughout a Christian's life, there is victory through Jesus (v. 25), and chapter 8 explains the life that the Christian has through the Spirit.

While no person—including a Christian—is perfected in this lifetime, we have assurance that "there is now no condemnation for those who are in Christ Jesus" (v. 1). No condemnation! Instead, we are alive in the Spirit (v. 11), adopted as sons and daughters of God (v. 15) and coheirs with Christ (v. 17). Furthermore, we have hope in this time of waiting (v. 23), help when our prayers are discouraging (v. 26), and ultimate victory over anything that would separate us from Christ (vv. 37–39). These promises are astoundingly, deeply encouraging for any Christian. Read through Romans 8 again to savor the goodness of our Lord and all that he has done for us!

Notes

Read: Summarize what you read today. Write down any questions you have about the passage.

Reflect: What do you learn about God in these chapters, and/or what do you learn about people? How do these chapters contribute to the overall story line of the Bible? What key themes are developed or fulfilled here? (Refer to the list at the beginning of the week for help.)

Respond: Is the struggle described in Romans 7 relatable to you? If so, in what way? What promises in Romans 8 are most precious to you right now? How would you describe the tension that exists between Romans 7 and Romans 8?

1 CORINTHIANS 15

As the early church grew and spread throughout Europe and Asia, Paul wrote letters to many of the churches he had started or visited. One such letter, 1 Corinthians, was directed to the church at Corinth and was full of encouragement and exhortations to the believers who were powerfully influenced by their pagan environment. Many of the problems addressed—immaturity, instability, infidelity, immorality, and others—continue to affect the lives of many churches today, and Paul wrote to remind them of the truth of the gospel and of their call to be holy. Paul's letters, which make up much of the New Testament, were written toward specific groups of people struggling with particular issues, and it is often helpful to understand the original problems in order to fully understand the purpose of the letter.

Toward the very end of this letter, in today's reading, Paul culminates his letter into a chapter on the significance and implications of the resurrection of Jesus. In a way, this letter provides the climax for many of the teachings he has set forth in this letter; in other words, the resurrection of Jesus—and someday, of ourselves—gives his previous teachings and directives ultimate meaning and purpose. He begins by summarizing what the gospel is (vv. 3–8) and why it is of "first importance" (v. 3). He then writes at length of the essential truth of the resurrection.

Some believers in Corinth were claiming that there was no resurrection of the body and that Christianity was a religion for this life only. This matches well with a current philosophy that it doesn't really matter whether Christianity is right or wrong; if it works for people, they should stick with it. But here, Paul explains that it matters *deeply* whether it is right or wrong and if there is a resurrection. He says that if no one is resurrected, then Jesus also was not resurrected; in that case, "faith is futile" (v. 17) and "all who have fallen asleep in Christ are lost" (v. 18). It was the resurrection that proved that Jesus was who he claimed to be and that truly showed his triumph over death and the grave. Furthermore, Paul argues, "If only for this life we have hope in Christ, we are to be pitied more than all men" (v. 19). Our very hope and faith depend not only on Jesus's resurrection but on ours as well.

In the verses that follow, Paul agrees with his critics that we don't know exactly what this resurrection will look like; we only know that it will be imperishable, glorious, and powerful" (vv. 42–44). But one thing we do know is this: "Death has been swallowed up in victory" (v. 54). In our time here on earth, we must face the inevitable reality of our own death and the eventual deaths of all those we love, provided Christ does not first return. This fact of death causes some to live without hope and consider everything meaningless, often leading either to excessive nihilism or hedonism. But we know that Jesus conquered death and that he gives us power over death as well, which gives us meaning in our lives and hope in our deaths.

Notes

Read: Summarize what you read today. Write down any questions you have about the passage.

Reflect: What do you learn about God in these chapters, and/or what do you learn about people? How do these chapters contribute to the overall story line of the Bible? What key themes are developed or fulfilled here? (Refer to the list at the beginning of the week for help.)

Respond: Why does Christianity hang on the essential truth of the resurrection? What implications does Jesus's resurrection and our eventual resurrection have for our lives today? How does today's chapter offer hope and encouragement in a fallen world?

38

PHILIPPIANS 2, COLOSSIANS 3

The book of Philippians, Paul's letter to the church at Philippi, is centered on themes of joy and humility. This encouragement is even more meaningful because of Paul's circumstances. He is writing this letter from prison.

Paul instructs his readers to be unified in mind, love, and spirit, much like Jesus prayed before his arrest and crucifixion (see reading for day 27). Similarly, he encourages them to be humble and to put others above themselves, just as Jesus did. He then expresses in poetic form how Jesus, "being in very nature God, did not consider equality with God something to be grasped, but made himself nothing" (vv. 6–7). These verses do not mean that Jesus misunderstood his role as God or thought himself beneath it and therefore rejected that claim. Rather, they express that Jesus did not insist that his full rights and status as God were something to be maintained by force. He chose to empty himself and humble himself even to death on our behalf. As a result, "God exalted him to the highest place" in order that "at the name of Jesus every knee should bow … and every tongue confess that Jesus Christ is Lord, to the glory of God the Father" (vv. 9–11). When we love sacrificially, when we do nothing out of selfish ambition, when we consider the needs of others above our own, we are simply following the example of Christ.

Similarly, in the book of Colossians, Paul's letter to the church at Colossae contains large sections of practical commands and encouragements to live a holy life. All of this is bound up in the truth of who Jesus is and what he has done (see Colossians 1:15–23 for an example in this particular book). But he never wanted his churches to forget that God has not saved us to simply go to heaven one day when we die. Rather, he invites us to be on mission in this world and to join in his plan of proclaiming the good news of his story. He calls us to be heirs with Christ, to be transformed by the Spirit and Word of God, to honor him by our words and conduct, and to be a light to those around us, ultimately bringing them into God's great story as well.

The chapter begins with the words "since, then," which indicate that the verses to follow stem from certain realities and backgrounds. Because we have already been "raised with Christ," our hearts and minds should be focused on things above (vv. 1–2). When we accepted Jesus's death and resurrection on our behalf, we died, and our lives "are now hidden with Christ in God" (v. 3). As such, our conduct ought to match that of one whose life is no longer their own.

The following verses use the imagery of taking off the old self and putting on the new self. The old self, or earthly nature, consists of anything that comes naturally to humans apart from the transforming work of Christ, such as "sexual immorality, impurity, lust, evil desires, and greed" (v. 6). Now, since we are God's chosen people, "holy and dearly loved," we are to clothe ourselves in a new self, consisting of qualities, such as "compassion, kindness, humility, gentleness, and patience" (v. 12). No matter what we do, we should forgive one another, love one another, be at peace with one another, and encourage one another through the Word of Christ, ultimately doing everything in the name of Jesus.

Notes

Read: Summarize what you read today. Write down any questions you have about the passage.

Reflect: What do you learn about God in these chapters, and/or what do you learn about people? How do these chapters contribute to the overall story line of the Bible? What key themes are developed or fulfilled here? (Refer to the list at the beginning of the week for help.)

Respond: What are some practical and theological implications of Paul's hymn in Philippians 2:6–11? How can you imitate Christ's humility in your home, community, church, or workplace? What do you think it means to set our hearts and minds on things above? What aspects of the old self are you currently working to put off, and what aspects of the new self are you currently working to put on?

39
· Day ·

HEBREWS 8-9

The entire book of Hebrews sets out to prove that *Jesus is better*—better than angels, better than humankind, better than Moses, and better than the priests and sacrifices of the old covenant. These chapters in particular gloriously bring together so many themes from days 1–20 of this study and explain how Jesus is the true definition of so many of the offices and ideas established in the Old Testament.

In the longest New Testament quotation from the Old Testament, chapter 8 quotes the prophesied new covenant from Jeremiah 31 (see day 20), the covenant that has come to pass thanks to the work and ministry of Jesus. When the author calls the old covenant "obsolete," he is referring to the Mosaic covenant with its system of laws, priests, and sacrifices (not to the entire Old Testament or even to the Abrahamic or Davidic covenants, which had largely been fulfilled in Jesus). Chapter 9 goes on to explain the full significance of Christ's death in terms of that old system. In short, the tabernacle's rules and regulations "were not able to clear the conscience of the worshiper … [they were] external regulations applying until the time of the new order" (vv. 9–10). Even the tabernacle and Most Holy Place themselves were copies and shadows of what was in heaven. So when Jesus died, he entered the *true* Most Holy Place—the very presence of God—as both *true* priest and *true* sacrifice "by his own blood, having obtained eternal redemption" (v. 12). God had allowed the blood of animals to make people ceremonially clean, so how much more would the blood of Christ purify people from the inside out! As the author triumphantly explains, "For this reason, Christ is the mediator of a new covenant, that those who are called may receive the promised eternal inheritance" (v. 15).

Furthermore, this sacrifice was better because it did not need to be repeated day after day or year after year. Rather, he appeared "once for all at the end of the ages to do away with sin by the sacrifice of himself" (v. 26). When he appears again, he will "bring salvation to those who are waiting for him" (v. 28). Creation was completed, rebellion was undertaken, and now true redemption was enacted. The only thing left in the story—restoration—has, in fact, already begun.

Notes

Read: Summarize what you read today. Write down any questions you have about the passage.

Reflect: What do you learn about God in these chapters, and/or what do you learn about people? How do these chapters contribute to the overall story line of the Bible? What key themes are developed or fulfilled here? (Refer to the list at the beginning of the week for help.)

Respond: Throughout this study, we have seen Jesus as the *true* king, the *true* prophet, the *true* temple, the *true* priest, the *true* sacrifice, and the *true* Israel. Which of these offices is most significant to you right now, and why? How has the Old Testament given you categories to understand who Jesus is? How can understanding these categories increase our love for him?

40

Day

REVELATION 21–22

Today we come to the end of the story. We have seen the overarching story line of creation, rebellion, and redemption throughout the Bible, and we have seen glimpses of the promised restoration in ourselves and in the world around us through the person and work of Jesus. But someday, that restoration will be complete. These last two chapters of the Bible offer a picture of the glorious hope that awaits believers. The imagery used here in this Holy City combines elements of Jerusalem, the temple, and the Garden of Eden, ultimately bringing the story full circle.

In this Holy City, the New Jerusalem, sin and its effects will be completely eradicated. God will be able to dwell with his people as he initially planned. No longer will rebellion and sinful nature separate his people from him. But as the prophet John writes, "Now the dwelling of God is with men, and he will live with them. They will be his people, and God himself will be their God. He will wipe every tear from their eyes. There will be no more death or mourning or crying or pain, for the old order of things has passed away" (21:3–4). Throughout the Bible, we have seen God take steps to live with his people—through the tabernacle and subsequent temple in the Old Testament, through the sacrificial system that gave people the categories to accept the death of Jesus on their behalf, and through the church that he built in his name. But now, at the end of all things and forevermore, God himself will be with them in a perfectly restored relationship.

When the angel measures the city, it is a perfect cube (21:16), thus reflecting the Most Holy Place in the tabernacle (see Exodus 26). Its gates are beautiful stones, its streets are made of gold, and the leaves of its trees bring healing to the nations. Whether this imagery is literal or symbolic, one thing is clear: God will reign with his people and the evil things of this world shall become undone. Everything will be as it was meant to be. And amazingly, wondrously, his people will see his face (22:4).

All of this is possible due to the love of God, the work of Jesus, and the invitation of the Spirit. Jesus reminds the readers that he is coming soon (22:12) and that he is the "Alpha and the Omega, the

First and the Last, the Beginning and the End" (22:13). Whatever we experience in this world, he was before it and he will be after it.

Ultimately, we are left with a choice. Will we heed the Spirit's invitation and come to Jesus for our salvation and for a restored relationship with the God who made us? The penalty has been paid on our behalf, and God is making an offer to us for him to be the center of our lives and the delight of our hearts. "Whoever is thirsty, let him come; and whoever wishes, let him take the free gift of the water of life" (22:17). Come!

Notes
Read: Summarize what you read today. Write down any questions you have about the passage.

Reflect: What do you learn about God in these chapters, and/or what do you learn about people? How do these chapters contribute to the overall story line of the Bible? What key themes are developed or fulfilled here? (Refer to the list at the beginning of the week for help.)

Respond: What aspects of the New Jerusalem described here are you most looking forward to? How are those who believe and those who do not believe contrasted in this chapter? At the end of Revelation 22—the last chapter in the Bible—Jesus says, "Yes, I am coming soon" (22:20). How does this truth impact your life now?

Days 36–40: Summary and Teaching

This is it: the final week! Throughout the past eight weeks, we have read twenty passages in the Old Testament and twenty passages in the New Testament to understand how God has been at work in the world and how he has revealed himself in his Word. We have looked at his faithfulness in covenants with his people and how Jesus fulfills every promise made from the very beginning. Last week, we saw how God began to use the church, through the power of the Holy Spirit, in this era of the new covenant that we now live in.

All throughout, we have been following the overarching story line of creation, rebellion, redemption, and restoration. After God created the world and everything in it, including humans, he declared it very good, and all was how it was meant to be. But the representatives of humanity, Adam and Eve, rebelled against God, as we continue to rebel to this very day. God gave hints of the redemption to come through covenants with Abraham, Moses, and David, through systems of priests and sacrifices, and through offices, such as kings and prophets. The Old Testament writers also spoke of an Anointed One, a Messiah who would come and save the people once and for all. When this Messiah, Jesus Christ, came into the world, he lived the life we should have lived and died the death that we deserved to die so that we might be reconciled to God. He enacted our redemption for us, and by his wounds, we are healed. With his resurrection, he inaugurated the promise of restoration. We now live in a time when the kingdom of God has already, but not yet, come, and in a time when restoration is already, but not yet, a reality. Pieces of this kingdom and this restoration were begun with the birth, life, death, resurrection, and ascension of Jesus, but we also await full consummation in the last days.

This week's passages highlight this tension where we currently live. Romans 7–8 reveals it in our daily battle between sin and the Spirit. First Corinthians 15 speaks of it when Paul explains the significance of Christ's bodily resurrection. Philippians 2 and Colossians 3 encourage us to live within it in a way that is honoring to God and to the new life that we have been given. Then our final two readings bring everything together. Hebrews 8–9 explains how Jesus is the fulfillment of everything set up in the Old Testament. And finally, Revelation 21–22 uses imagery from Genesis 1–2 to describe the true recreation, or restoration, of all things. For one last time, let's dive into these passages and see how God has spoken to us in his Word.

In Romans 7, Paul sets forth an incredibly relatable argument about the struggle with sin. He explains that one of the purposes of the law is to make us aware of our sin. Everyone, including you and me, is sinful without even knowing the law, just based on our own consciences alone. Put another way, we all have standards of goodness and morality that we can't even live up to, regardless of our relationship with God or lack thereof. But when the law put words to that sinful nature, it condemned its hearers. Earlier in Romans 6:23, Paul wrote that "the wages of sin is death," and the good law set forth in the Old Testament revealed sin, which led to death. In verse 15, the struggle is described this way: "I do not understand what I do. For what I want to do I do not do, but what I hate I do." This tension of *wanting* to obey God and walk in a way that is upright, moral, and holy is contrasting with the reality of *acting* out of sin, and this tension is present in our lives as well. We have the best of intentions, but often we fall short; we have a deep understanding of what we should do, but we don't do it; we know that we need to stop doing what hurts us, but we feel powerless to do so. In the depths of confusion and despair, Paul cries out, "What a wretched man I am! Who will rescue me from this body of death?" And then the beautiful answer. "Thanks be to God—through Jesus Christ our Lord!" (vv. 24–25).

And then, we see this powerful contrast in 8:1. "Therefore, there is now *no condemnation* for those who are in Christ Jesus." The law, as mentioned earlier, was a good thing, but it was never intended to bring salvation. Here in verse 3, Paul says that "what the law was powerless to do" was accomplished by God in "sending his own Son in the likeness of sinful man to be a sin offering." The law could point out, condemn, and even bring up sin, but it was powerless to save. Indeed, that had never been its intention. The sacrifices and offerings of the OT had been set up to allow a sinful people to dwell with a holy God, and their very existence acknowledged that the people would not be able to keep all of the commandments and stipulations of the law. There would need to be provisions for when they failed. But when Jesus came as our great and perfect and final sin offering, he "condemned sin in sinful man," and through faith in his life, death, and resurrection, we can now live according to the Spirit.

These chapters indicate the reality of sin in our lives. When we place our faith in Christ, we do not automatically begin to live perfect lives in every area. Our struggles and our sin remain. But God is working on us, in us, through us. Hebrews 10:14 puts it this way: "By one sacrifice he has made perfect forever those who are being made holy." When we place our trust in Jesus, we are declared righteous because of his work on our behalf. This event is called justification. But at the same time, we are being transformed into his likeness through the Holy Spirit. This process is called sanctification.

Romans 8 is a beautiful and encouraging reminder of this reality, this tension, in which we live. We have been set free from the penalty of sin. We are being set free from the power of sin. And we will be set free one day from the presence of sin. Until that day, we are children of God, calling out, "Abba, Father," through the Spirit. That same Spirit intercedes for us when we don't even know what to pray. And that same Spirit gives us assurance of God's love and God's faithfulness, reminding us that "neither death nor life, neither angels nor demons, neither the present nor the future, nor any powers, neither height nor depth, nor anything else in all creation, will be able to separate us from the love of God that is in Christ Jesus our Lord" (8:38–39). *God* is the one who has initiated, chosen, and enacted our salvation, and he will continue his good work despite our failings. We strive to walk in the Spirit, and God enables us to do his will. The already-but-not-yet tension is present, but we who have been chosen are secure in it. According to verse 30, our glorification is as secure as though it has already happened.

We turn next to Paul's explanation of the hope and significance found in Jesus's bodily resurrection in 1 Corinthians 15. First, he clarifies what he means by the gospel, or good news, by which we are saved. According to vv. 3–8, the gospel is this: "that Christ died for our sins according to the Scriptures, that he was buried, that he was raised on the third day according to the Scriptures, and that he appeared to" the disciples and to many others. All of this occurred as it had been written. For Paul and for his readers, the hope of what Jesus had done was grounded in the entirety of the Word of God. Many of the passages Paul likely had in mind here were ones we have looked at in this study: Isaiah 53, the sacrificial and priestly system, the Passover, and others. God's grand plan in effect from the beginning is given equal weight to the events we so often sing and talk about: the death and resurrection of Jesus.

Speaking of this resurrection, Paul turns to address a false teaching that there would be no resurrection of the body. Paul soundly defeats this argument since the entire gospel turns on this reality. Verses 13–19 indicate that if there is no resurrection at all, then Christ hasn't been raised from the dead, and if Christ hasn't been raised from the dead, we are still in our sins. Jesus would have been one more offering, one more substitutionary atonement, but he wouldn't have been the once-for-all sacrifice for sins and reconciliation to God without his resurrection. Verse 17 states that without that historical, bodily event, our faith would be "futile"; verse 19 goes one step further and says that "if only for this life we have hope in Christ, we are to be pitied more than all men." If there is no hope of resurrection, then our faith is delusional. False hope is more dangerous than no hope at all. Some people might ask, "What's the harm in believing something, even if it's not true, if it gives you hope?" Paul here argues that there is *great* harm and we are to be pitied in our delusions.

But, he says, Christ *has* been raised from the dead. All of the people he mentioned in the first few verses of the chapter—himself included—can testify to that truth. And more than that, Christ's resurrection is a pledge, a deposit, to guarantee our own resurrection. We have hope beyond today, beyond this life! Verse 22 brings up an idea we have seen before, that of Jesus as the true Adam. Both served as a representative of humanity, but whereas Adam brought death, Christ brought eternal life. What is more, this bodily resurrection truly fulfills the Old Testament covenants to Abraham and to David, when God promised an everlasting covenant with Abraham's descendants and a son of David to sit on the throne forever. If Jesus were not raised, and we were not raised, these promises would be useless, and God himself would be a liar. As Jesus was the firstfruits of those who had risen from the dead, so we too shall be raised. This promise of restoration is absolutely crucial to our faith!

The final part of this chapter addresses those who understandably want more details about this resurrection. What will it be like? What will our bodies be like? While we do not and cannot understand all of the specifics, the body that is raised will be different from the one we experience now—greater in glory, splendor, and immortality. One thing is true from these great expressions of our hope that death will be swallowed up in victory: our faith cannot simply be spiritualized away. The Christian hope is not in an ethereal God with a baseless religion and feel-good faith. It is a way of life grounded in a historical event, with hope for the future in a physical resurrection and restoration of all things. One of the greatest scandals of the gospel message is that God became flesh. He came among us, walked this earth, and got his feet dusty. Jesus's incarnation teaches us that we cannot label everything physical as evil and everything spiritual as good. And once again, we see the tension between what is already and what is not yet. We have this hope, but it has not yet become reality. But whatever the resurrection itself is like, we know that we will be raised imperishable, we shall be changed, we shall live as God's people, and God himself will be our God. Thanks be to God!

The next chapters continue to speak of the tension we live in in this current age until Christ comes again in power and in glory. Philippians 2 and Colossians 3 are parts of a series of letters called the epistles that Paul wrote to various churches he had started or heard about. In each of these epistles, he first reminds his readers of the truth of who God is and what he has done on their behalf. Whether in several verses or several chapters, he always opens with the gospel and their resulting identity in Christ. Only then does he go on to talk about practical living amid that new identity. Even though we didn't read those initial chapters as part of this study, understanding their order is extremely important. God never calls his people to live in the Spirit without first empowering them by that Spirit through Jesus's life, death, and resurrection.

With that in mind, we turn to Philippians 2. The main point of this epistle is a plea for unity and for a spirit of thankfulness, as Paul himself is thankful for a gift that they had sent. In his admonitions to the church in this chapter, he continually bases these things in the example of Jesus. He encourages them to consider others over themselves, to be humble, and to look to the interests of others. And in order to ground this admonishment, he writes one of the great early hymns of the faith, explaining how Jesus himself—God the Son!—did not hesitate to act in these ways as well.

He goes on in verses 12–13 to encourage them to "work out [their] salvation with fear and trembling, for it is God who works in [them] to will and to act according to his good purpose." This is a prime example of that tension; we work out our salvation, yes, but it is also God who is working in us to act in that way. We act, God acts, and our actions are so intertwined as believers that it is almost impossible to separate them. We are called to certain actions, and we also have the power to do them. We pursue them, and we also rely on God. Paul ends this chapter by telling brief stories of two other followers of Jesus, Timothy and Epaphroditus. They are both held up as examples to follow, indicating to us that in this tension, we can also look to the examples of others. We are not alone in this walk with Christ!

Colossians 3 follows in a similar vein. We should set our minds on things above and on Christ, and we should pursue a life that matches up to the new identity we have in Jesus. In the Old Testament and in the gospels and teachings of Jesus alike, belief is tied with obedience. If we truly believe the gospel and who we are as a result, we will live lives that reflect that. There is no place for a Christian who claims to know and love Jesus yet walks consistently in the sinful nature. Instead, as God's chosen people (once again indicating the order here: we are saved, therefore we obey; we do not obey to be saved), we should clothe ourselves with "compassion, kindness, humility, gentleness, and patience" (verse 12). Forgiveness, love, peace, thankfulness, and the Word of God should characterize our actions and our speech because of who we are now. Once again, we are not yet perfect, and it is truly a daily walk with Christ as we pursue everyday faithfulness, but as we internalize his Word and live by his Spirit, we play a part in the kingdom of God continuing to push into our world.

So now we come to our final two passages of this study, both of which wrap up our forty-day overview of the Bible perfectly. First, let's look at Hebrews 8–9. The entire book of Hebrews (well worth an in-depth study in itself!) sets forth an argument that Jesus is *better*—better than previous revelations from God, better than angels, better than humankind, better than Moses, and better than the promises of the Old Covenant. He himself has fulfilled every one. These two chapters in particular highlight how and why he, as high priest of the new covenant, is superior to the priests and sacrifices that came with the old covenant.

Chapter 8 starts out by reminding us that the entire old system was a "copy and shadow of what is in heaven" (v. 5). Moses had specific instructions about the building of the tabernacle, the priestly order, and the sacrificial system because they were a pattern of the true reality. As we saw throughout the first half of this study, the old covenants were holy, righteous, and good and were set in place to foreshadow and prepare the people for the coming Messiah. They were saved by faith, just as we are today, but their relationship with God needed to be constantly maintained by external rituals and sacrifices to allow a sinful people to dwell with a holy God.

But now that Jesus has come, he has received a better ministry, a better covenant. Verse 6 says, "But the ministry Jesus has received is as superior to theirs as the covenant of which he is mediator is superior to the old one, and it is founded on better promises." It is better than the old one because it is the fulfillment, whereas the old was a promissory note; it is the reality, whereas the old was a preparatory shadow. Indeed, as verse 7 indicates, if the old covenant had been enough to save, there would be no need for a new covenant. But even within the Old Testament itself, we find a sure statement that the old covenant will be replaced by the new. The author quotes at length from the passage in Jeremiah we studied earlier, indicating that a new covenant would come, one that would be written on the hearts of the people and would allow them to know God personally with total and unequivocal forgiveness of sins based on a better sacrifice.

Chapter 9 continues this argument and goes a bit more in-depth about what this actually looks like. First, the author reviews some of the specifics of the old covenant tabernacle and priestly system, from the placement of the furniture to the duties of the high priest. He specifically mentions the Day of Atonement, which we also studied earlier, when the high priest could enter only once a year after making sacrifices for his own sins so that he could then make sacrifices for the sins of the people. As verse 8 explains, "The Holy Spirit was showing by this that the way into the Most Holy Place had not yet been disclosed as long as the first tabernacle was still standing." These external regulations applied only until the time of the new order.

But when Christ came, he was both "high priest" (verse 11) and ultimate sacrifice, since "he entered the Most Holy Place once for all by his own blood, having obtained eternal redemption" (verse 12). Rather than mere external cleansing, the blood of Christ provides internal cleansing and ultimate, eternal salvation for those who believe in him! He is the "mediator of a new covenant" (v. 15), and we now live in the glorious light of this new covenant, promised by Jeremiah hundreds of years before the birth of Jesus. Just as the old covenant required blood to go into effect, this new covenant also required blood. But this blood, the blood of Jesus, our great and ultimate Passover Lamb, was shed for us, and we are saved by nothing but the blood of Jesus once and for all. The author concludes these amazing chapters by reminding his readers that when Jesus appears a second time, it will not be to bear sin (he has already done that) but to bring salvation to all who are waiting for him.

So with that, we turn to our final passage: Revelation 21–22, a foretaste of that Second Coming, when Jesus brings full and complete restoration and salvation to all who are waiting for him. We cannot understand the story of the Bible without understanding the ending, as it is the ultimate goal of our faith. So much more is happening in the gospel than just our personal salvation. Isaiah spoke of a "covenant of peace" (54:10)—one last covenant characterized by total well-being that flows from a right relationship with the living, Sovereign Lord. Even the end of *our* story is not the end of *the* story.

These final two chapters of the Bible have many parallels to the first two chapters of Genesis, before the rebellion of humankind against God. The two pairs create the "covers" of this greatest story of redemption. In both, humans are representational. In other words, as man goes, so goes the world. When humans fell into sin, the created world also fell; when humans are restored, the world is restored as well. (We also saw hints of this in Romans 7–8 this week.) This new heaven and new earth, particularly the New Jerusalem, combine elements from the Garden of Eden, the temple, and Jerusalem—all places that were real but also symbolic and significant. Each was a place where God dwelt with his people in close proximity and represented how things were meant to be. The twelve gates of the city echo the number 12 in both the number of the tribes of Israel and the number of Jesus's apostles. Furthermore, the city measures as a perfect cube. The only other place in the Bible whose measurements are a perfect cube was the Most Holy Place of the tabernacle, where the high priest made sacrifices for the people on the Day of Atonement. And as we just saw in Hebrews 8–9, this Most Holy Place has now been made open to all of us through the blood of Christ. When Jesus died, the curtain of the temple—the one setting apart that Most Holy Place—was torn in two from top to bottom. And now, in Revelation, the place where believers dwell intimately with their God—with "no more death or mourning or crying or pain" (v. 4)—echoes this wide-open Most Holy Place for us, for eternity.

Whether the language of Revelation is literal, symbolic, or historical, one thing is clear: this is true and complete restoration of all things. The river of life flowing through the middle of the city once again echoes the garden imagery of Eden as well as other places in the Old Testament, like Isaiah and Ezekiel. God is honored and glorified in this place, and his people reign with him. There is *healing*. There is *joy*. There is *peace*. We will see our God face-to-face and will live and reign alongside him forevermore in total restoration of all things. And all will be as it was meant to be.

And one last time, note the continuity with the Old Testament. Some of the last words Jesus says in the Bible are "I am the Root and the Offspring of David, and the bright Morning Star" (Revelation 22:16). What was promised thousands of years ago has now come true. By God's gracious plan, a descendant of David will reign on the throne forever and ever.

This study has taken us from the first chapter of the Bible to the last as we examined the unity of the scriptures and the story line of how God has revealed himself in his Word. We have seen how the types and covenants of the Old Testament paved the way for the ultimate fulfillment in Jesus. We have studied how we, as the church, now live in this age of already-but-not-yet tension. And we have explored in detail God's great story of creation, rebellion, redemption, and restoration.

Thank you for joining me in this study. My hope and my prayer are that this has deepened your understanding of God's Word and led you to be in awe of him. I encourage you to continue to study the riches of God's Word. We have barely scratched the surface of the treasures found in its pages. Our God has chosen to reveal himself in the pages of a book, so may studying that eternal book be one of the greatest joys of our lives. Whatever you do next, I pray that God will give you a heart to love and study his Word and to live in light of it.

Most of all, I pray that Jesus has been exalted in our study and in your minds, to the glory of God the Father. Jesus, our great high priest, has come, and we can be reconciled to God through his life, death, and resurrection. Jesus is coming again soon, so let me close with the words of Revelation 22:17. "The Spirit and the bride say, 'Come!' And let him who hears say, 'Come!' Whoever is thirsty, let him come; and whoever wishes, let him take the free gift of the water of life." Come, behold the Lamb of God who takes away the sin of the world. Come and see Jesus through the unified Word of God!

NEXT STEPS

The past forty days have taken you through forty key passages in the Bible. You have experienced God's overarching story line of creation, rebellion, redemption, and restoration in its pages. You have read of the ways that the Old Testament prepared categories, people, and promises that led to Jesus. You have seen threads and repeating themes that appear again and again throughout the Bible. And you have glimpsed the glory of God in the gospel of Jesus Christ.

This Word of God is living and active (Hebrews 4:12). It is always relevant, always true, and always needed. Now that you have a better understanding of how the whole book fits together, you may want to dig deeper into a particular passage or book with the help of a commentary or study Bible. Or you may want to start a reading plan that takes you through the whole Bible.

Here are some resources you might find helpful:

- **D. A. Carson's *For the Love of God*:** This is a reading plan and accompanying short commentary to read two or four chapters per day from different parts of the Bible. Used every day at four chapters a day, this will take you through the Old Testament once and the New Testament and book of Psalms twice in a year. It is also easily modifiable for a longer period, such as two chapters a day over two years. Carson offers a small and helpful commentary on one of the chapters but keeps the focus on the scripture. His teaching and work have been incredibly influential in my understanding of how the Bible fits together.
- **Book recommendations: *According to Plan* by Graeme Goldsworthy, *Far as the Curse Is Found* by Michael D. Williams, or *Even Better than Eden* by Nancie Guthrie:** These books are introductions to biblical theology or understanding how the Bible fits together as a whole. They trace several themes from beginning to end. Parts of this forty-day overview emphasized some of those themes, and all of these books have helped to train my thinking.
- **BibleProject:** BibleProject offers free videos, classes, podcasts, and more to help people experience the Bible as a unified story that leads to Jesus. I would especially recommend their videos introducing each book of the Bible as well as their podcast series on Paradigms for Reading the Bible, originally released in fall 2021. See all of their excellent resources at bibleproject.com.

- **The Bible Recap:** This includes a plan to read through the Bible chronologically in a year, with short daily podcasts to help you understand each day's reading. Check out thebiblerecap.com for more information.
- **YouVersion, Blue Letter Bible, or Scripture Memory apps:** These free apps allow you to continue your study of God's Word with study tools, different versions of the Bible, community connections, and daily email opportunities.

Whatever you choose, be realistic with your time, learning styles, and needs. Set aside a time and place for simple, consistent meeting with God in order to know and love him more. If you fall behind, don't give up and don't be discouraged. Try again the following day. This is hard work, but knowing God is worth it. Pastor and theologian John Piper wrote, "Loving God is most essentially treasuring God—valuing him, cherishing him, admiring him, desiring him. And loving him with all our mind means that our thinking is wholly engaged to do all it can to awaken and express this heartfelt fullness of treasuring God above all things." May we continue to know God through his Word, love him with our lives, and bring glory to him in everything, for he is Most High and most worthy of all of our praise.

ACKNOWLEDGMENTS

I first learned about the Bible from my parents and from so many at Grace Polaris and Worthington Christian schools. During my time with Cru at Ohio State and in Eastern Europe, I learned how to put the pieces together into one story. I had the initial idea for this study during an outreach at Redemption in Charlotte, I began to write it while at Cross City in Columbus, and I first taught it at Refuge in St. Charles. So many people in all of those places have taught me so much. Thank you to everyone who has been a part of this. Thanks especially to Susan, Josh, Katy, and Leslie for providing invaluable feedback during the editing process. And thank you, Joel, for letting me revisit the same issues just one more time.

SAMPLE BIBLE STUDY CALENDAR FOR A GROUP SETTING

You should complete the five days of reading and reflection for the week *before* the meeting date. For example, when you go to meeting 2, the discussion will cover days 1–5, so you should already have read those chapters and completed the questions.

Meeting	Content
Meeting 1	Introduction
Meeting 2	Days 1–5
Meeting 3	Days 6–10
Meeting 4	Days 11–15
Meeting 5	Days 16–20
Meeting 6	Days 21–25
Meeting 7	Days 26–30
Meeting 8	Days 31–35
Meeting 9	Days 36–40

RESOURCES AND REFERENCES

Alexander, T. Desmond, et al., editors. *New Dictionary of Biblical Theology.* Downers Grove: IVP Academic, 2004.

Barker, Kenneth, et al., editors. *NIV Study Bible.* Grand Rapids: Zondervan, 2002.

Carson, D. A. *For the Love of God, Volumes I & II.* Wheaton: Crossway, 1998.

Goldsworthy, Graeme. *According to Plan: The Unfolding Revelation of God in the Bible.* Downers Grove: IVP Academic, 2002.

Hamilton, James M. *What Is Biblical Theology? A Guide to the Bible's Story, Symbolism, and Patterns.* Wheaton: Crossway, 2013.

Kaiser, Walter C., and Douglas J. Moo. *Five Views on Law and Gospel.* Grand Rapids: Zondervan, 1996.

Piper, John. *Fifty Reasons Why Jesus Came to Die.* Wheaton: Crossway, 2006.

Richter, Sandra L. *The Epic of Eden: A Christian Entry into the Old Testament.* Downers Grove: IVP Academic, 2008.

Schreiner, Thomas R. *The King in His Beauty: A Biblical Theology of the Old and New Testaments.* Ada: Baker Academic, 2013.

Williams, Michael. *Far as the Curse Is Found: The Covenant Story of Redemption.* Phillipsburg: P&R Publishing, 2005.

Wright, Christopher. *Knowing Jesus through the Old Testament.* Downers Grove: IVP Academic, 2014.

Printed in the United States
by Baker & Taylor Publisher Services